Soviet Ethics and Morality

*A Study of The Russian
Institute of Columbia University*

Soviet Ethics and Morality
by Richard T. De George

Ann Arbor
The University of Michigan Press

The Russian Institute of Columbia University
sponsors the Studies of the Russian Institute
in the belief that their publication contributes
to scholarly research and public understanding.
In this way the Institute, while not necessarily
endorsing their conclusions, is pleased to make
available the results of some of the research
conducted under its auspices. A list of the
Studies of the Russian Institute appears at
the back of the book.

Preface

Marxist-Leninist ethics and communist morality stem from and are part of the Western tradition. In recent years the Soviet Marxist-Leninist literature on ethics has grown to significant proportions, and in the Soviet Union the importance of communist morality to the building of communism has become a prominent theme which has been emphasized with increasing vigor by Soviet leaders. Yet in the West Marxist-Leninist ethics and communist morality are relatively unknown aspects of Soviet philosophy and life.

By writing the pages which follow I hope to fill an informational gap by objective exposition. But I shall also evaluate the developing Marxist-Leninist ethics and communist morality to see what, if anything, may be learned from them, and what, if any, are their shortcomings and pitfalls. Throughout I shall attempt to indicate where and how contemporary Soviet developments in ethics and morality compare and fit in with those taking place in the West.

The first portion of this book will be concerned exclusively with Soviet writings in the field of ethical theory. I shall present and critically analyze the Soviet Marxist-Leninist position with respect to the origin, nature, and function of morality, the meaning of ethical terms, the justification and derivation of moral virtues, and the status of moral values. Where possible and where it will be helpful, I shall translate Soviet ethical jargon into comparable terms more current in contemporary Western ethical literature. I shall treat the Soviet position as a philosophical one and attempt to evaluate it as such, bracketing —to the extent possible—the ideological overtones and intent which are often found mixed in with Soviet philosophical discussions.

In the second portion of this book I shall turn to Soviet

official morality. In 1961 the Communist Party of the Soviet Union promulgated the Moral Code of the Builder of Communism, a code which listed the basic principles of communist morality which Soviet citizens are expected to live by. It was highly publicized in the Soviet Union, it has been taken as a model by some of the other countries of Eastern Europe, and it is used in some instances as the basis for social norms, enforced both by public opinion and by "comrade's courts." Dictated from above, it is an ideological tool, and part of my endeavor will be to consider it as such.

The Code itself attempted to fix and emphasize certain moral traits which the Communist Party believed necessary for Soviet citizens to exemplify if the Soviet Union is to achieve the communism which the New Party Programme promised them in the not too distant future. Some of these traits are those customarily held to be essential for the functioning of any society; some are peculiar to the special society which the Soviet citizens are said to be building.

I shall critically examine the Code, the morality it preaches, and the ideal it champions. In some ways the Code presents an ideal type, which the people of Soviet society are to attempt to reach in their lives. For those who use it to pattern their lives and actions, it serves as something of a blueprint. If it becomes a model of human conduct accepted by the Soviet people, it may eventually guide the lives of millions of people in the world in which we live. It thus deserves careful scrutiny, both for its possible positive aspects which others may emulate, and for its possible negative aspects which may fall short of or negate values which man in his history and in his better moments has espoused as his moral ideal. To some extent the choice of different ideals rests on different views of man and different ways of conceiving his life; where this is so, I shall attempt to clarify the choices at stake. Where factual claims are involved, explicitly or surreptitiously, I shall try to distinguish these from the value judgments with which they are often mixed.

Throughout I have consciously and purposely limited myself to the official and quasi-official philosophical literature on ethics and morality published in the Soviet Union, and to the popular literature based thereon. Though there is reason to believe that some Soviet philosophers may hold views (existentialistic, positivistic, Marxist revisionist or other) at variance with the official Marxist-Leninist position, such views never see print. Similarly, though a somewhat different morality may be implied in some contemporary Soviet fiction, any counter-code contained therein is still extremely amorphous, its formulation requires tools and methods different from those I propose to use here, and its investigation would in fact be the subject for another whole study. Similarly, I shall make no attempt to answer the empirical question of how successful Soviet leaders have been in inculcating the new moral principles in the Soviet people.

In confining myself to the extant philosophical and quasi-philosophical literature, I shall be dealing with the generally accepted framework within which Soviet moral philosophers work. There are some differences among Soviet philosophers, as we shall see, on specific issues, interpretations, and formulations. But they all accept a basic common orientation and framework, which I shall refer to as either the Soviet or the Marxist-Leninist position or view. Though similar in many ways to other ethical positions, it constitutes a distinctive position of its own.

My critical comments are not intended to show that the Soviet ethical position is philosophically untenable, though they will point up areas where more critical analysis, clarification, and development are required. Nor shall I, as a rule, try to second-guess Soviet philosophers and so possibly confuse what their position currently is with what it might become. There are many ways that a Marxist ethics might go, and no one can predict how the Soviet Marxist-Leninist position will in fact develop. It is part of my hope that from this and similar studies some dialogue may emerge between diverse philosophical schools, some understanding may develop concerning divergent value schemes, and some common ground may be found either by philosophers dealing with similar problems or by peoples sharing common values or ideals.

This manuscript was written while I was a Senior Research Fellow at the Russian Institute of Columbia University. To the members of the Institute go my thanks and appreciation for their support, assistance, and the use of the Institute's facilities. A grant from the Ford Foundation funds given to the University of Kansas in support of international studies made possible additional time for research and helped me see this work through its early stages. To the members of the Institute of East European Studies at Fribourg, Switzerland, I am especially indebted for their encouragement when this project was initially conceived and gradually began to take shape during my stay there.

R. D. G.
July 1968

Contents

Chapter I: Introduction   1

Chapter II: The Basis of Soviet Ethics   13

Chapter III: Good and the Moral Ideal   35

Chapter IV: Freedom, Duty, and Moral Evaluation   57

Chapter V: The New Moral Code   83

Chapter VI: Moral Inculcation and Social Control   105

Chapter VII: Ethical Criticism and Moral Crisis   127

Notes   153

Bibliography   175

Index   183

Introduction

Soviet Marxist-Leninist ethics claims to be based on the writings of Marx, Engels, and Lenin, and to be the only true, accurate, and hence orthodox interpretation and development of the ethical position and moral values presented in these writings. In fact, however, Marx, Engels, and Lenin had very little explicit to say on moral philosophy as such. Their writings in this domain are both meagre and extremely ambiguous. The history of philosophy has seen many divergent systems built on the Marxist legacy—some more or less Kantian, some more or less Nietzschean, and today in the countries of Eastern Europe some more or less existentialistic. All of them can with some justification be called Marxist, all can claim Marx as their inspiration, and all can point to texts of Marx or of Marx and Engels in support of their positions.

The very proliferation of Marxist views on ethics by both West and East Europeans seems to support the assertion that there is no one coherent body of doctrine that can be unambiguously called Marx's ethical position. His views changed and developed throughout his life. The moral views explicitly or implicitly contained in *The Holy Family* or in the *Economic and Philosophic Manuscripts of 1844* cannot be equated with those contained in *Capital* or in the *Critique of the Gotha Program*.

If, as Marx thought, morality was part of the superstructure of society, then no special theory concerning it was necessary. As a product of a society's basic economic conditions, it would change as these conditions changed. Marx was emphatic in his rejection of moralizing. But this did not prevent him from championing certain values and from morally condemning capitalism, the oppression of man by man, exploitation, and alienation. He had a vision of man, who in some future, plentiful society would be able to enjoy his full, all-round development in harmony and in cooperation with all his fellow men. He charted a path which he thought would lead—perhaps inevitably—to this glorious, future, communistic state of man. But this path in some central ways negated the values he championed for his future society.

In the Marxist ethical literature Marx's influence is decisive and still influential. Engels attempted to formulate an ethical position in *Ludwig Feuerbach* and *Anti-Dühring*, but it was in each case clearer in its rejection of anything that might be called an eternal morality, than in its formulation of any positive position. Lenin, despite the claims of Soviet philosophers[1] brought little of an ethical or moral dimension to Marxism except to adopt the Nechaevan dictum that what helps the revolution is moral and what hinders it immoral, what helps the building of communism is moral and what hinders it is immoral —a formula which in fact forms the basis of the new Soviet Moral Code of the Builder of Communism.

The extent to which the Soviet position is Marxist or Leninist or revisionist is an historical and academic question. However it is classified it must stand or fall on its own merits. Yet many of its problems have their roots in Marxist doctrine and become less intelligible if separated from their historical antecedents. A position is automatically neither true nor false simply because Marx held it; but the fact that Marx held a certain position is sometimes more significant in explaining why it is held today by Soviet philosophers than its truth or falsity as judged by some non-Marxist criteria.

One of Marx's great moral insights—and one he shared with others of his day and of later days—was his perception of the dehumanization of man which accompanied the industrial revolution. His criticism of the existing social order, and of the exploitation and oppression which accompanied that order, cut deeper than many other moral views which rested content with alleviating suffering rather than condemning its cause. Marx's moral condemnation, however, became intertwined with his economic views, with his conception of man and with his ideal of a future society—not all parts of which were equally sound and defensible. He equated the division of labor and the existence of private property with man's alienation. The equation was dubious. He thought that by doing away with the former two, society could do away with alienation as well. But he failed to demonstrate that all alienation came only from the division of labor and the existence of private property. He failed to inquire whether there were other causes for it, and whether different societies might not suffer from different forms of alienation. He envisaged a society of plenty, but failed to examine whether such a society was compatible with the abolition of the division of labor which historically accompanies industrialization and with the growth of knowledge which demands further and further specialization.

Marx seems to be the champion of the freedom and creativity of man at the same time that he preaches a collectivist theory of man that subordinates the individual to society, individual good to social good, and human freedom to collective freedom. Hopefully, the individual and social good, individual and social aims will coincide. But that they will is a hope. When they are *made* to coincide by social engineering or manipulation, it must necessarily be at the expense of individual choice and freedom.

Marx's humanism conflicts with his notion of the amoralism of historical necessity. For on the one hand man's lot is to be improved because of what he is and deserves to be; on the other hand, whatever is, necessarily is as it is. Marx's view of freedom is ambiguous to the extent that it relates to individual freedom: freedom seems to be a quality or capability which man has, and which must be developed individually. But for Marx it is also something which is won for the individual and *given* to him. Similarly, Marx's attempt to provide security for man must be reconciled with his desire to give men maximum scope for their free activity.

Marxism promises a society of plenty in which justice will flourish for all. But the means it advocates to achieve this end lack the justice the end requires. Marx saw more clearly than most moral philosophers the responsibility of man for history and for his social system; but he also undermined this responsibility by his deterministic view of history in which history unfolds as a play. The most man can do is hasten the inevitable or slow it up. He can never change it significantly. The individual, moreover, is ineffective as compared to the masses, who are the only real forgers of history.

These and similar problems, goals, ideals, condemnations and confusions are taken over by the Soviet philosophers and become topics for discussion, clarification, dilemma, obfuscation, or for solution from above.

Attempts at constructing a Marxist ethics in Russia date back to the period of the 1890's; other abortive attempts appeared in the 1920's.[2] But it is only since the 1950's that an ethical literature of any consequence has developed in the Soviet Union. Prior to that time, evidently, the dominant official position was that there was no need for a separate discipline dedicated to the study of the development of morality, since morality as a form of social consciousness changed as the economic conditions of society changed. By the 1950's however, it had become clear that despite the fact that the economic conditions of the Soviet Union had changed quite radically since 1917, social consciousness had changed comparatively little. Private ownership of the means of production had been replaced by state ownership, thus precluding—at least in theory—the exploitation of one individual by another. New relations of production had been forged. But the new man of Soviet society had not yet emerged. Crime was still prevalent, as was drunkenness, parasitism, and rowdiness, and such "bourgeois" traits as acquisitiveness and jealousy were all too obviously present. The new man had not yet appeared. He was still to be formed.

The development of a Soviet ethical literature was a complex phenomenon and can be explained as a result of several interrelated factors. The first of these is the general revivification which took place in Soviet philosophy after 1947.[3] At a conference called by the Central Committee of the Communist Party of the Soviet Union, ostensibly to discuss Professor G. Alexandrov's *History of West-European Philosophy*, A. A. Zhdanov, a member of the Politburo, spoke in Stalin's name. He criticized Soviet philosophers for their lack of productivity and for failing to apply Marxism to the problems of Soviet society.

The conference was followed by the founding of the Soviet philosophical journal, *Voprosy filosofii,* and by a significant increase in philosophical activity, which continued and became even more vigorous after the death of Stalin. This general loosening of the Soviet philosophical scene made possible more philosophical investigation than had previously been the case under Stalin. The way was thus cleared for developing a body of Marxist-Leninist ethical literature.

A second factor was the emphasis Stalin had placed on the active role of the superstructure, especially in his 1950 articles on the linguistics controversy.[4] The superstructure of Soviet society, he claimed, did not merely reflect developments of the economic base. It exerted a positive active force in the society's development. Thus parts of the superstructure, such as morality, could play an active role in the development of Soviet society. This doctrine provided a justification for studying morality as a particular object of investigation.

The legitimacy of this approach was further justified by the doctrine of the "relative independence" of various parts of the superstructure. According to this, the parts of the superstructure are affected not only by changes in the base but also by their previous stages of development. A particular philosophy, or ethical theory or moral code could not therefore be adequately understood merely by studying the economic conditions of a society. The antecedent philosophies, ethical theories, and moral codes would also have to be considered. As this doctrine, which has its basis as far back as Engels' letter to Bloch,[5] came into prominence, the break of ethics (as well as other disciplines) from historical materialism gained support and justification. While previously all forms of social consciousness (morality, art, religion, etc.) had been treated only to the extent that they fell under the laws of historical materialism, in the 1950's ethics and other disciplines came to be recognized as distinct fields of investigation.

These factors set the scene for the development of Soviet ethics. But by themselves they are insufficient to explain the rapid growth of a body of ethical literature in the Soviet Union. Two other factors are significant, both of them related to the needs and demands of the Communist Party of the Soviet Union. The first was the necessity of refuting both bourgeois ethical theories and those revisionist ethical positions which were being spun on the basis of Marx's early writings, particularly the *Economic and Philosophic Manuscripts of 1844*.[6] Refutation was and continues to be a dominant theme in Soviet ethics. An initial impetus for theorizing in this field, its objective was primarily negative. But it also had some positive by-products. By seeking to deny the humanism of the early Marx to the revisionists, the Soviet writers claimed it for themselves and perforce made humanism a more central part of Marxist-Leninist ethics than it might have otherwise been. By attempting to refute bourgeois theories Soviet theoreticians were also forced to find answers to questions neither they, nor Marx, nor Engels had previously considered. Refutation thus accounts in part both for the development of a Marxist-Leninist theory of values[7] and for the development of some metaethical questions.

The second and even more significant demand of the CPSU concerned the inculcation of communist values in the Soviet people. Together with the notion of the active role of the super-structure the notion of the moral-political unity of the Soviet people came to prominence. At the same time Party leaders realized more clearly that moral incentives could be applied for purposes of social control, for increased productivity (by making work for the good of society a moral obligation), and for fostering public support for internal and external governmental policies which were justified as moral as well as politically necessary or expedient. More of the Soviet ethical literature is devoted to the teaching and spreading of Communist morality than to any other theme. This trend has, if anything, increased since the 1961 Party Program and the announcement that the Soviet Union had entered the stage of the building of communism, with its achievement predicted "in the main" by 1980. While force and terror had been used as instruments of social control in the Soviet Union during most of the reign of Stalin, it became evident by the 1950's and especially since Stalin's denunciation in 1956, that if communism is to be built it must stand not on a basis of terror but on a more tolerable and popularly acceptable basis. One important feature of this new basis is the stability which a society of citizens who live according to the correct moral code would have. Morality was seen by the leaders of Soviet society as a possible instrument to replace the rule of force and eventually perhaps even the rule of law, since it afforded internal control of the individual by himself according to certain norms, and the spontaneous correction and disciplining by his fellow citizens of anyone who violates the code. The propagation and justification of the new moral code fell to the philosophers, as did the task of working up a theory of morals which would explain and support the derivation of the moral code. Other aspects of the problem of the inculcation of moral norms and values were given to sociologists, social psychologists, and pedagogues.

The comparatively recent development of a body of Soviet ethical literature in part explains the relative philosophical crudity of some of its formulations when compared with discussions in the Anglo-American journals. Moreover, since the Soviet ethical position has been developed within the Marxist framework, it is not surprising that it often sounds like and resembles ethical theories of the nineteenth century more than those of the twentieth century in the Anglo-American literature. Yet many of the questions it deals with are questions basic to any moral theory.

Since neither Marx nor Engels nor Lenin had left behind any explicit and well-formulated moral theory, Soviet philosophers had more scope in developing a Marxist-Leninist ethics than they would have had if circumscribed tightly by some classical formulation comparable to Lenin's copy theory of knowledge in the field of epistemology. That Marx's writings made available an ample basis for the creative development of an ethical theory is born out both by some of the earlier Marxist revisionist theories and by the writings of such contemporary Marxist philosophers as Lukacs in Hungary or Kolakowski in Poland. But ideology predominated over philosophy and caution over creativity, and as a result the development of Soviet ethical theory has been slower, less original, and in many ways less philosophically developed than it might have been.[8]

Because of the nature of morality the moral philosopher has traditionally been faced with two different and sometimes conflicting tasks. Since morality is one of the bases of social stability, many moral philosophers, from Aristotle on, have seen part of their task as consisting of an analysis, defense, and justification of the morality of their societies. It was not up to them to preach morality or dictate morals, but in some way to make sense of morality. Aristotle attempted to formulate the ethics of the enlightened Athenian citizen; Descartes, who was so daring in the realm of speculative thought, cautioned against scepticism, even as a method, in the moral realm; Kant sought a basis for morality, but by no means a new morality; Bentham and Mill sought certain reforms, but on the whole defended the existing moral norms and argued that men had implicitly been utilitarians all along and that anyone following utilitarianism had common human moral experience to fall back upon for the greater part of his moral choices.

Together with the defense of the existing moral system, a task which they sometimes performed unwittingly, moral philosophers have also often been called upon or have volunteered to judge the morality of particular actions or classes of actions, to untangle difficult moral problems, and to help decide moral issues. Though this facet of the moral philosopher's work has come to be associated with casuistry and is disclaimed by many philosophers, it is still practiced by some, and a great many laymen seem to feel that moral philosophers should help resolve such perplexities as the morality of atomic stockpiling or of population control.

Besides the task of justifying and of sometimes interpreting the existing morality, the moral philosopher, as a philosopher, also often attempts to uncover presuppositions, clarify the meanings of terms, and render a moral system or theory unambiguous and consistent. But this aspect of his work is sometimes at odds with the defense of the existing moral order of society. Thus Nietzsche undermined the foundation of Western culture and morality, or at least attempted to call into doubt the validity of contemporary values and the basis of Christian morality; Kierkegaard in his own way criticized prevailing Christian morality as un-Christian; Marx condemned capitalist society as immoral. Each defended as higher and more worthy of man's allegiance a morality other than the one of his society. Other philosophers have called for reform in the name of the consistent application of principles, or have sought to show that certain arguments which were purported to support certain actions were specious (as deterrence being a justification for capital punishment, or determinism being an excuse for any action whatsoever, or religious belief being the only basis for any morality at all).

The endeavor of the moral philosopher has thus often been felt to pull in two ways, the one in support of the morality of his society, and the other in support of rational consistency, which sometimes undermined parts of the moral order of that society. Some philosophers have emphasized one or the other aspect of moral philosophy. Others claim that the proper philosophical task is simply the clarification of moral terms, a task which is neutral with respect to any existing moral practices.

The Soviet moral philosopher is faced with the dual task of moralizer and philosopher. But his efforts in the direction of philosophy at the expense of the existing system are doubly circumscribed. First of all he is committed to the Marxist-Leninist framework. His moral theory must be consistent with Marxist theory in general, with Marx's moral judgments, such as his condemnation of capitalism, and with his theory of historical and social development. Secondly, the Soviet philosopher's philosophical activity must always be subordinate to the Party's ideological requirements and can never be at variance with them.

The Soviet moral philosopher is most often told in general terms what problems need solving and to which questions he should turn his attention. He is expected to develop, explain, and defend communist morality—not question or undermine it. The general directives come from the Communist Party Program, Party pronouncements, or speeches by Party theoreticians. These in turn are translated into more specific directives in editorials in the philosophical periodicals, or in projects drawn up by the philosophical institutes. Those interested in moral philosophy are expected to adhere to or at least to consider these directives seriously. The development of an idea or theme by an individual philosopher is not completely precluded, but in the field of ethics this has thus far been a relatively rare occurrence. In the few instances when it has occurred (as with Tugarinov's *O tsennostiakh zhizni i kul'tury*), it has always taken place within the prescribed ideological limits and has upset conservative philosophers more than the accepted communist moral system which they defend and support.

The new communist morality which is being promulgated, defended, and preached to the Soviet people finds an uneasy resting place with many Soviet citizens; the morality is new and many of its values are not compatible with those of the past. Russia has emerged very rapidly from a primarily agrarian country to an industrial giant; many of its people have not kept up with the changes. As a result of Marxism some values of an industrial society are prized—the plenty that comes from mass production, the control that accompanies an advanced technology—and some have been scorned. Both the Soviet leaders and the Soviet theoreticians have found it no easy task to preserve the positive aspects of industrialization while avoiding its negative aspects, and to impose these positive values upon the agrarian values which still have deep roots in the Soviet Union.

The place of the individual in society is a topic ambiguously treated by Marx and his followers. Under communism, supposedly, personal and social interests and needs will coincide. But until they do, social needs take precedence over personal needs in Soviet theory and official practice. Convincing Soviet citizens of the moral primacy of the social realm over the personal realm remains one difficulty for Soviet leaders. Another consists of attempting to reconcile the free all-round development of the individual which was Marx's ideal, with the authoritarian, controlled society which Soviet leaders deem necessary to achieve the end of communism.

The tension which the Soviet philosopher experiences in attempting both to uphold and defend communist morality and to follow arguments and principles where they lead, is a kind of tension which he shares to some extent with other moral philosophers. But his subservience to ideological demands and his forced operation within the confines of the Marxist-Leninist framework take their toll in stifling his originality and creativity. The tension between personal and social interests and needs is one similarly shared by other systems. But the imposed necessity of justifying present authority for future freedom, present sacrifice for future plenty adds a dimension which results in a paradoxical value system, many aspects of which still require clarification.

In the first three chapters which follow I shall examine Soviet ethical theory—its basis, structure and content; this will be followed by a consideration of Soviet morality—the new moral code and its implications for Soviet society.

Chapter II

The Basis of Soviet Ethics

Soviet ethics is in some ways similar to pragmatism, to utilitarianism, to ethical relativism, to Darwinian evolutionism, to natural law ethics, and to Christian ethics. But it is reducible to none of these and forms a distinctive theory of its own. It is part of the Marxist-Leninist philosophical system, and relies heavily on the materialist conception of history; it is historical in its approach to morality, but not entirely relativistic. It denies that morality has any extraterrestrial source, and claims to take a "materialistic" approach to morality. But it does not therefore extol base values or deny the validity of moral ideals. It is dialectical and attempts to balance, account for, and interrelate the objective and subjective, relative and absolute, temporal and eternal, class-bound and universal aspects of morality. It forms a piece with Marxist theory as a whole, with dialectical and historical materialism, Marxist political economy, and scientific communism. The concern of this chapter will be to get an overview of Soviet ethics as a whole, and to examine the basis of Soviet ethical theory, its fundamental orientation, and its conception of what "morality" means.

Ethics, according to Soviet ethical theory, can be broadly characterized as the theory of morals.[1] Marxist-Leninist ethics, as opposed to other ethical theories, is not merely one theory of morals among others, but, its practitioners boldly claim, it is the *science* of morals.[2] If "science" is defined as "a systematic body of knowledge," then the claim is that Marxist-Leninist ethical theory is the only true account of morality. This claim, which we shall examine shortly, is defended negatively by showing how all other theories are in some ways deficient, and positively by showing how Marxist-Leninist ethics can handle all the pertinent facts about moral phenomena. As a science of morality it attempts to account for the origin and development of morals, to

13

define the essence of morality, to clarify the nature of moral judgments and of moral ideals, to explain the role of morality in society, to relate the laws of social development to the lawlike moral progress of mankind, and to uncover the principles and norms of communist morality.[3] Soviet moral philosophers refuse the distinction between critical ethics (or metaethics) and normative ethics, claiming not that these are not two functions of ethics but that the two are so intertwined as to be inseparable.[4]

Morality, according to Soviet ethical theory, is a form of social consciousness.[5] As such it follows upon social being. "Social being" is defined as "the material life of society, the production of material goods and those relations (in a class society they are class relations), into which men enter in the process of this production. Social consciousness consists of views, notions, ideas, political, legal, aesthetic, ethical, and other theories, philosophy, morality, religion, and other forms of consciousness."[6] Thus morality is one of a number of forms of social consciousness and, as all forms of social consciousness, it is held to reflect a form of social being. The position stated by Marx and Engels, is repeated by Soviet philosophers: "We set out from real, active men, and on the basis of their real-life process we demonstrate the development of the ideological reflexes and echoes of this life-process. The phantoms formed in the human brain are also, necessarily, sublimates of their material life-process, which is empirically verifiable and bound to material processes. Morality, religion, metaphysics, all the rest of ideology and their corresponding forms of consciousness, thus no longer retain the semblance of independence. They have no history, no development; but men, developing their material production and their material intercourse, alter, along with this their real existence, their thinking and the products of their thinking. Life is not determined by consciousness, but consciousness by life."[7]

According to the Marxist position man as man emerges only with society, and both his language and his consciousness are social products.[8] Men are distinguished from animals by the fact that they *produce* their means of subsistence.[9] Since what a being is depends on the way he expresses his life, what men are depends on what and how they produce. "The nature of individuals thus depends on the material conditions determining their production."[10] Man's social being, then, refers to the means by which man in society produces his life. This is equivalent to his means and modes of production, and the relations of production in his society. The "material" conditions of his life are roughly speaking the economic conditions of his life. For Marx and his followers these conditions are basic and determine the conscious life of society which is built upon them.

"Social consciousness" is a somewhat ambiguous term. Whether social consciousness consists of the ideas and theories held by a society in some collective way or whether it is the sum of the ideas and theories held individually by the members of a society is still a debated issue in the Soviet Union. On either interpretation the term refers not to all forms of consciousness, but only to certain forms, such as morality, religion, and philosophy. As consciousness is held to be a reflection of being, so social consciousness is said to be a reflection of social being. This means that the content of the various forms of social consciousness depends on the economic basis of society. Since consciousness is an attribute properly ascribable only to individuals, it is always individuals who *have* social consciousness. It is only as members of a class, however, and not in their individuality, that they have *social* consciousness—just as it is always as a result of belonging to society that they are men at all, and not as a result of their own individual activity.

What is reflected in social consciousness is not the means and modes of production directly, but the social relations which are built on the relations of production. These social relations are consciously given formulations and justifications, which result in the various forms of social consciousness. The relation of social being and of social consciousness is not simple, but complex. Since the details of this relationship constitute the subject matter of historical materialism, ethics, which studies one form of social consciousness, namely morality, leans heavily on historical materialism, as part to whole. The rise and development of morality, according to Marxist-Leninist theory, is a particular instance of the rise and development of social consciousness in general.[11]

By "morality" is meant "the totality of principles or norms (rules) of men's conduct which regulate their relations to one another, to society, to a certain class, to the state, country, family, and so on, supported by personal conviction, tradition, education, the force of public opinion of a whole society or of a certain class."[12] The definition is of course much too broad and includes much that would not ordinarily be considered part of morality, such as certain social formalities, or regional customs. But though morality must be distinguished from other forms of social consciousness, the vagueness of the Soviet definition is in part intentional and not merely the result of an absence of analytical acuity. For morality is often not easily distinguished from nonmoral customs either by the philosopher or by the moral agent or by his fellow men. The line between custom and morality is often a thin one, and the distinction between an act done from habit and a moral act is often a highly debatable one. The vagueness is also relevant to the origin of morality, which, according to Marxist-Leninist theory, was not received whole from any extra-human source, was not inborn in man, but like man himself evolved slowly.

The Marxist-Leninist approach to morality is thus from the outset an historical one. Morality is not to be defined a priori, nor is it to be obtained by an analysis of current linguistic usage alone. For the very notion of what constitutes morality has varied, developed, and changed; the variety, development, and change must all be accounted for and must not merely be passed over in silence or defined away.

Morality, according to the Soviet view, emerged slowly in human society, as slowly as human consciousness and human society emerged. As man came to live in society, he found that the very mode of his life, his association with other men, imposed certain demands upon him. These demands consisted of certain required actions and ways of acting if men were to work and live together. For collective aims could be achieved and a community life lived only if men cooperated with one another, helped one another, and could trust one another at least to a minimal degree. As these ways of acting became accepted in a community they developed into customs or customary forms of conduct. It is from these customs that morality developed.[13] The particular customs which were adopted depended on the life of the given community or society. Different communities found themselves in different conditions of life and so adopted different customs, which they felt would help them achieve their aims, ranging from simple survival to the continuance of an increasingly complex social life. Since customs vary and since morals were based originally on customs, it is only natural that we should find a wide variety of moral norms and prescriptions from culture to culture.

The findings of anthropologists are pertinent here and constitute facts which must be acknowledged and incorporated into any ethical theory which hopes to account for the origin, diversity, and development of morality. Soviet ethical theory admits the full strength of findings by such anthropologists as Margaret Mead or William Sumner. But the diversity of mores, based on differing physical or productive conditions, though a part of the explanation of differing and apparently contradictory moral codes, does not substantiate the position of ethical relativity espoused by Sumner and others. It may well be that infanticide or the killing of one's aged parents is considered moral in one society and immoral in another. But to argue from this to the claim that morality is completely relative either from society to society or from person to person is, in the Soviet view, to take a false step. The anthropological approach to morality is only part of the truth. It correctly emphasizes that moral norms vary and that there is no single, eternal moral code that has been binding on all men at all times and in all places, either in fact or in principle. But the anthropologists see only the relative aspect of morality, and fail to see its objective side. Their position must therefore be enlarged and corrected.

According to the Soviet view, mores and customs vary from place to place and age to age. But they are never arbitrary. They arise from the physical and economic conditions of a society with a certain necessity, and so are to that extent objective. Certain actions will in fact help a society maintain itself in existence and progress; other actions will in fact impede its progress and perhaps lead to its extinction. Which actions will have which effects is determined not by the whim, fiat, or will of any individual in the society, or by all the individuals together, but by the objective conditions of the society. In seeking to advance their interests, interests which are in large part determined by the necessity of keeping themselves alive, the members of a society may well make false starts or initiate harmful customs. The simple existence of a custom, therefore, is not sufficient to show that what the custom enjoins is good or right for that society and what it forbids is bad or wrong. "Right" does not necessarily mean "what my society approves of." In each case the criterion is the objective conditions of the society, and the belief that certain actions will advance society's interests and others will impede them.

The relativity of moral judgments depends on two factors. One is that conditions differ in different societies. The other is that societies or individuals may erroneously (subjectively) think that a certain action will help achieve their aims, when in fact it will not. The first aspect of the objectivity of mores and of morality is that they are based on the objective conditions of the given society; the second is that they are based on the interests and needs of that society which are compatible with its objective conditions.

Marxist-Leninist theory asserts that the step from mores and customs to morality is historically a step in the development of human consciousness. Thus certain customs or norms which are or are considered most essential to a society are formalized into rules and become moral prescriptions. These are often worked up into a system or formulated into a moral code, which is consciously taught and transmitted from generation to generation. While customs constitute practical conduct, morality is socialized, formalized, abstracted from customs and expressed as imperatives or commands. Usually the moral imperatives are not, to use Kantian terms, hypothetical imperatives or imperatives of skill. They are categorical imperatives. They receive their categorical force because of the basic necessity for the continuance of progress of society. Formulated by a society, they are usually expressed by that society in universal terms. They carry the weight of social pressure and public opinion, and are so inculcated in the members of society that they become internalized and appear as the voice of conscience. Their categorical form has an objective base; but moral imperatives must always be considered in their historical context, in their social environment, and in their concrete form, and not merely in their empty formal aspect. Together with Kant moral imperatives can be considered as coming from reason; but Kant's mistake, Soviet philosophers insist, was to make morality a formal, a priori affair, springing from reason. In fact, however, reason itself developed historically; and while insight into the objective demands of society is rational, it is never empty, formal, or abstract. They admit no formal principle as necessary for morality as such.

As society became more complex and the division of labor was introduced, the primitive clan or collective developed into a class society, in which men were divided into an exploiting minority and an exploited, oppressed majority.[14] The position of Marx is here taken over by Soviet philosophers *in toto*. The morality of a slaveholding society, like the morality of any class society, is not uniform throughout the society but dual (or multiple). Since each class is opposed to the other, their interests do not coincide but rather conflict. As Nietzsche also saw, what is good for one is evil for the other; what helps one oppresses the other. But the dominating class attempts to impose its morality on the dominated class. The morality which serves the interests of the ruling class becomes the morality which is preached, taught, and backed up by the power of the state and by religion. Morality became in the hands of the rulers a device for social control and stability, for protecting their interests and the status quo. Ethics, or the theory of morals, developed gradually in Greece. Philosophers, conscious or unconscious representatives of the ruling class, spun out ethical theories which attempted to formalize and justify the ruling morality. Philosophers did not create a new morality, but gave voice to the existing morality. Thus, Aristotle, one of the greatest thinkers of ancient times, says that some men are born to be slaves, and considers neither slaves nor women to be persons in their own right. Soviet philosophers quote Aristotle here not to condemn him, but to make clear the true function of morality and a traditional function of the moral philosopher.

The relation between the moralities of the dominant class and of the dominated class is ambiguous in the writings of Marx and Engels. According to one interpretation, each class acts as it is forced to by its circumstances. The rich act to protect their interests; they preach one morality and follow another. The poor and the oppressed may for a time listen to the morality preached to them by the leaders of society, but they are forced to act otherwise. Each class acts as it does necessarily; and consequently any discussion of the morality or immorality of actions becomes superfluous. Morality is reduced to necessity.

Soviet philosophers, however, reject this interpretation both because it leads to a denial of morality and because it fails to account for the actual historical conflict of moralities in the development of society. While it is true, they claim, that each class acts in its own interests, several distinctions must be made. The ruling class through the schools, churches, and state apparatus preaches a morality (e.g., it is wrong to steal private property) which protects the interests of its members. They do not live by or follow this morality, but either live by none (and so are amoral) or by another which has its own rules according to which they might be judged immoral (e.g., it is permissible to steal from the oppressed by exploiting them, but it is immoral to steal from one's peers). The morality which is officially preached is followed by some of the oppressed; or at least some try to follow it until forced to do otherwise. They then either act amorally or they adopt a new set of standards by which to live and according to which they judge themselves or each other (e.g., it is permissible to steal from the rich, but not from the poor or from those poorer than oneself). Each class, therefore, though forced to act in certain ways, formulates a moral code based on the actual conditions and interests of its members, according to which they are judged. Though based on necessity, morality is on this interpretation not reduced to it. As slavery became unprofitable because of advancing means and modes of production, the Marxist-Leninist position continues, slave society gave way to feudal society. With feudal society came feudal morality, sanctified by the Church. Feudal society in turn led to capitalist society, which brought with it bourgeois morality and opened wide the road for the struggle of the proletariat for freedom.

This proletarian morality, which condemned oppression and exploitation, was a morality which grew out of the conditions to which the proletariat had been subjected in capitalist society. It expressed the interests of the working masses, and was formulated and brought to the consciousness of these masses initially by Marx and Engels, and then by their followers. Its principles, it is claimed, led to the October Revolution in Russia, and to the establishment of a classless society, free of the exploitation of one individual by another. As the economic base of socialism developed in the Soviet Union, there developed new social relations, and so a new morality. Ultimately, when communism is achieved, communist morality will become fully developed and reign triumphant. Since a communist society is a classless society, there will be only one morality, in which the interests of all humanity are expressed, and in which individual and social interests will coincide.

This in brief is a sketch of how, according to Marxism-Leninism, morality originated and has developed. For completeness two additional clarifications should be made. First, though the Marxist-Leninist position claims that morality follows upon and is ultimately determined by economic conditions and changes in a society, the relation is neither direct nor simple. Because of this, morality (and also ethics, and other forms of the super-structure) enjoys a certain "relative independence" in its development. This independence is manifested in three ways: in the lag of morality behind social being, in the projection of morality beyond social being, and in the continuity in the development of morality.[15]

The lag of morality behind social being reflects the fact that often economic conditions change more rapidly than the ideological superstructure, including morality, which is built upon them. This is due to several factors. One is that moral norms, learned young and having a certain categorical quality associated with them, have built into them what might be called an inhibitory quality. The fact that they are related to certain economic conditions and ways of life is not clear to those who follow established moral norms or codes, and they are reluctant to give up old ways for new. This is especially true in stable societies where certain traditions have been followed for generations. Changes in the way of life bring about changes in the morality. Though this often happens slowly it is sometimes accompanied by a crisis in the morality of the community, or a break between generations with fathers not understanding their sons.

The conservative function of morality and its use by the ruling class to preserve its position and the status quo also inhibits moral change. Where the status quo is threatened by changing conditions, the ruling class, reluctant to give up its position and privileges, is the last to admit the changes, and continues to propagate the ideas and morality favorable to itself.

A third reason for the lag of moral change behind changing conditions of life stems from the nature of ideas themselves. Men can separate ideas from their origins and consider them as independent entities or as an independent sphere or realm. Ideas can consequently be discussed, believed, and followed, despite the fact that they are no longer relevant.

The projection of morality beyond social being results from the fact that morality is related to society's economic base and to the real objective needs of the society. Since it is possible to see developing trends before they are fully developed, it is possible to foresee certain needs of social development before they are forced upon one. As a result, moral ideals which act as guides to a society may be developed. Thus, the Marxist-Leninists maintain, Marx and Engels and Lenin foresaw the necessary development of capitalism into socialism and communism, and in foreseeing the development of the economic base they were able to some extent to see the changes in morality which would accompany it. Similarly, the new Soviet moral code states the qualities and principles which the building of a communist society demands, and is based not only on present demands but to some extent on a projection into the future. Whether Marxism actually has uncovered the laws of social development is not at issue here. The point is simply that man is capable of seeing trends and of projecting into the future, and that this ability is the basis for part of the relative independence of morality from a society's economic conditions.

The continuity of morality helps to explain the form which morality and moral codes take at any given time. For no society simply throws overboard its past customs, traditions, or morality, but gradually changes them. It replaces some customs, modifies others, establishes new ones. For a proper understanding of the morality of any society at any given point, it is necessary to understand its previous development. It is not possible to look at the economic conditions of a society and deduce its morality from that. For many of the customs, moral and otherwise, of a society, are closely related to previous customs of that society. A wide variety of different customs are compatible with any given economic base. A society may simply not accept certain aspects of its morality from the previous generation but may to a limited extent consciously examine other moral ideals and attempt to revivify or propagate certain aspects of them.

The upshot of the relative independence of morality is that the Marxist-Leninist explanation of the origin and development of morality becomes much more flexible. It is able to account for changes in morality, for the continuance of what seem to be exceptions to the rule when morality does not change with the base, and for the existence of a multiplicity of moralities which may exist in a single differentiated society. In the latter case, for instance in the United States, it is possible to claim that there is not only the morality of the bourgeoisie and of the proletariat, but also carryovers of feudal, Christian, slave-holding and perhaps other moralities, as well as various combinations of these.

A second addition to the basic Marxist-Leninist account of morality is the claim of an "all-human" morality. This claim has two parts. The first is that common to the moral codes of all societies—or at least of the overwhelming majority—there are certain simple, common elements which are necessary to the conduct of any society.[16] These common norms include a general prohibition against murder (or unjust killing, despite variations of interpretation), and against lying, and general injunctions to keep one's promises, and so forth. Each moral code is thus formed on the basis of human experience, and expresses the objective needs of the community, some of which are common to all societies that survive or prove viable. The second claim is that this minimal aspect of all-human morality which forms a core of any morality is developed into a full-fledged all-human morality in communist morality.[17] The claim here is that communist morality expresses the interests of all mankind, or at least of its overwhelming majority. Thus it is not only the morality of the future communist society, but, as there will be no reason for its being superseded by another morality, it will answer the needs of all men in a classless society.

Now the explanation of morality which we have presented so far has a certain plausibility and validity, though it suffers from a considerable amount of vagueness of detail, and raises some questionable claims about the future. We shall have the opportunity to investigate these in more detail later on. But a question that arises immediately is: what is peculiarly ethical about the considerations we have seen so far? If we grant that we have a plausible theory about the origin and development of customs, we may still insist that we have said precious little about morality as such. If the origin of morality goes back to mores and customs, does this mean that morality is reducible to these? If morality comes from the demands of the physical and economic conditions of a society, does that mean that each society's morality is as good as any other society's? Is it possible to speak about better or worse, good or bad in any distinctively moral sense, or is morality reducible to utility, to what works for a society? Are some aims of society better than others, and how does one choose? Is there such a thing as moral progress as well as changes in moral codes, and if so, how is this to be measured? Soviet ethical theory attempts to answer these questions, and it is to these answers that we now turn.

While morality originates in mores and customs, Marxist-Leninist theory holds that it is not reducible to these. The precise distinguishing traits are left vague, though morality is distinguished generally as a distinct sphere of social conscious-

171.0947 D363a

The Basis of Soviet Ethics

c./ **25**

ness, is described in distinctive categories, and is said to include distinctive ideas and feelings which are properly called moral. Morality, according to one Soviet definition, is the aggregate of the rules and norms which regulate the conduct of men in society.[18] Moral rules and norms differ from legal rules and norms both in their form of promulgation and in the form of restraint and punishment they impose. Legal rules and norms are officially formulated and propagated in detail and are enforced by the power of the state. Moral norms are not necessarily officially formulated and promulgated by the state and are enforced by the power of public opinion and individual conscience. Legal norms enforce and strengthen what society has already achieved in social relations; moral norms underline not only what is, but what *should* be. Thus unlike anthropology, psychology, and sociology, ethics is concerned not only with factual descriptions and analyses but also with norms, ideals, and moral values.[19]

At least one distinctive aspect of morality is that it involves ideals or values which *should* be striven for or realized. The description of the development of morality in terms of the needs of social development which we saw above was value-free. Although societies have different moralities, depending on their differing conditions and interests and aims, Marxist-Leninist ethical theory does not stop here. Although each class and each society expresses its own interests and develops its own morality, not all interests or aims are equally worthwhile. While the entrepreneur may justify his exploitation of his workers and defend a morality which safeguards his property and keeps his workers subservient, his exploitation is condemned as unjust by proletarian morality. The matter is not settled by merely stating that the different classes have different interests, and that the moral evaluation of acts is relative to these interests. The interests themselves can be evaluated. There are two different issues involved here which should be kept distinct. The first is whether at each stage of social development each class or group can evaluate its own morality in terms of its own criteria; the second is whether in the light of some ultimate criterion one can judge and evaluate competing ideals, interests, and moralities.

A society's morality is ultimately determined, according to Marxist-Leninist theory, by its physical and economic conditions. These impose certain demands on the members of the society if it is to survive and develop. Thus a certain morality is imposed upon the members of any given society. If an individual member fails to realize his duty, his action, if performed in accordance with what he thinks is his duty, may be subjectively right, though objectively wrong. Similarly a society may think that certain norms are objective demands which must be followed for its social progress, and it may be mistaken in this regard. Individual members of the society may see more clearly what is in fact required and propose or attempt to bring about reforms, which are more in accord with the objective needs of the society. This is one way a society or its members may judge their own moral code or rules.

The discrepency between the actual moral rules a society has adopted and those which would be most conducive to its fullest social development may be due to lack of knowledge or insight. It may also be the result of the lag of morality behind social being. Conditions may change, and what were correct norms at one stage of a society's development may be incorrect at another stage. In a class society failure to change certain norms may be indicative of simple nonmoral failure to make the change or it may itself be indicative of an attempt on the part of elements of society to prevent a change or to preserve a state of affairs from which they profit at the expense of others. If their profit at the expense of others was necessary for society's development, then, according to Marxist-Leninist theory, their actions were moral by the objective criterion of society's needs. When other alternatives become available, however, they may become immoral in preserving the old system despite changing needs. Thus slavery in the days of the Greeks may well have been necessary for the development of society at the stage of economic development then available. When it was no longer necessary, and even detrimental, then the morality of slavery changed. It became recognized as generally wrong, even if some individuals sought private gain by continuing to trade in slaves. For the objective criterion of morality, according to Soviet theory, is always the good or development of society as a whole, not of some of its individual members.

The second question we raised was whether the goals of any society can be evaluated in comparison with the goals of any other. Here Soviet ethics leans heavily on the materialist conception of history and the Marxist notion of the progressive development of mankind. According to Marxist theory, human society has been progressing from primitive to slave-holding to feudal to capitalist to socialist society and it will continue to develop towards the ideal social system, which is communism. Similarly, the criterion according to which one is to judge social aims and goals is the ultimate criterion of communism, which in Marxist-Leninist theory is the ultimate moral ideal of mankind. The Soviet defense of this position and an evaluation of it will be our concern in Chapter III. But the present point is that Soviet ethics does present an ultimate ideal in terms of which the ends of any given society may be morally evaluated. Moreover, it holds that there is only one moral end, since it is the end of mankind as such, and that this end is not simply the subjective end of Soviet or communist society, but the ultimate objective ideal for all societies.

We can now classify Soviet ethical theory according to some of the more common distinctions and classifications usually made in contemporary Western ethical literature. Though Marxist-Leninist ethics admits certain relative aspects of morality and accounts for the diversity of moral codes which have developed at different times and places in human history, it is basically an objectivist ethical position. It claims that the moral norms for each society are the objective norms necessary for its social development. Though objective conditions vary, however, it also has an absolute objective norm or ideal in terms of which it evaluates the ideals of different societies as more or less progressive, depending on whether or not, and to what extent, they tend towards the ideal of communism. To say that the ideal is absolute, however, does not imply that it either has any extraterrestrial source, such as God or Reason, or that it is eternal or always existed or had some form of reality. As an ideal it appeared only with the appearance of man, and it came to be consciously formulated as an ideal only slowly in time, and in particular only with Marx and Engels.

Besides being objectivist, Soviet ethics is also naturalistic, that is, it claims that "good" is definable in terms of certain natural properties. An analysis and discussion of this claim will be one of our concerns in the next chapter. Finally it is a teleological ethical position. There is an ultimate criterion of morality, the achievement of future communist society, in terms of which a judgment of moral worth is made and on the basis of which obligations are derived. "Right" and "duty" as we shall see in some detail in Chapter IV are defined in terms of good in general, and the ultimate good in particular.

It is less easy, however, to specify exactly what type of teleological theory the Marxist-Leninist position is. For while it shares some aspects of the traditional self-realization type theories, it also resembles natural law and utilitarian theories to some extent. Its basis is a view of man and of society which is in some ways unique.

Like natural law theories it holds that man can find out what is right and what is wrong by looking at nature. This helps explain how men in different societies came to discover the common simple laws necessary to every society. But Soviet philosophers do not generalize this position; and unlike most natural law theories they would hold that some acts, like infanticide, may well be right in one society and wrong in another. The Soviet position is closer to a type of utilitarian position, which judges the rightness or wrongness of an act by its consequences. Thus an action could be said to be right if it tended to produce the greatest good on the whole, where "good" was synonymous with the achievement of communism. What leads to communism is good, what hinders it is bad. But whereas in a strictly utilitarian system the utilitarian method should be used for deciding, among other things, what type of social system will yield maximum welfare, communist morality already claims to know this answer and has arrived at it by other than utilitarian methods. Thus the Soviet ethical position seems to resemble most closely the position of self-realization, though of a special kind.

The Marxist-Leninist position judges both individual actions and social systems by their tendency to promote or hinder the achievement of communism. Communism is man's ultimate end, because only in communism will man become what he was truly meant to be. This claim involves three steps which we find worked out in Soviet ethical theory: 1) a technique for describing man's actual condition; 2) an ideal view of what man should be in terms of which man's actual condition at any given time in history can be measured; and 3) a justification of this ideal view as the moral end of mankind.

The Soviet view of man differs from many Western views in that it is collectivist instead of individualist. Man as man appears only in society. Apart from society we cannot speak of individual men. The Marxist-Leninist analysis of what man is and should be is always an analysis of social man. We must not begin with an individual who merely expresses himself in a society with other individuals, and who finds his true self in some sense by himself, for there is no such individual. Marx stated the position succinctly in his sixth thesis on Feurebach: "the human essence is no abstraction inherent in each single individual. In its reality it is the ensemble of the social relations."[20] The mistake of the early French socialists, Marx and Engels maintained, was to look for the nature of man in individual men, isolated from other men. The mistake of the idealists was to look for the essence of man in consciousness. But the only correct place to start in the search for man's nature is with man as he actually exists; and this is in society, together with other men.

For Marx, man is a natural being who is to be defined by the way he acts.[21] Distinctive about him, as we have seen, is the fact that he works and produces his subsistence. How he works therefore determines what he is. At any given time in history we can see what man is by looking at his social relations. He acts in society, never alone. Man's sociality is not something added to his other qualities, such as consciousness or reason. It is an intrinsic part of him and infects his consciousness, his reason, and any other quality that may be named as distinctive of man.

Since man is what he does, and since he acts in society, helping to produce the means of his subsistence, he can be most adequately defined by describing the social relations of society, i.e., by describing the way he is related to the means and modes of production and the way he is related to his fellow men. A society's means and modes of production and the resulting social relations are never the result of the action of any one man. Each society inherits these and at best modifies them slightly in passing them on to the next generation. Thus, while it is true that man makes himself what he is and that he makes his society, he always does so collectively, never individually. The existentialists err when they say that each man makes himself individually or in the solitude of his lonely choice; for the possibilities he has to choose from are determined by the society in which he lives. The mistake of many philosophers is that they take what man is in their own society as a mark of man's nature as such, failing to see that man's nature changes and develops throughout history.

The Marxist view of man which we have thus far presented, however, is value free. We can describe the nature of any man in any society by describing the ensemble of the social relations of that society. No one society is better than any other society; they are merely different. To this descriptive aspect of man, Marx and his followers then add a valuative aspect of man, according to which man, collectively taken, has a certain ideal nature which he is to fulfill. It is against this ideal that human progress in general can be measured, and it is against this ideal that man's moral progress can similarly be measured.

The human ideal which the Marxist-Leninists maintain is the only true one was formulated by Marx and Engels.[22] The condition or state of society in which man enjoyed ideal social relations and so realized his true nature, was termed by them "communism." The lack of precision in the formulation of the meaning of this term, while in certain respects understandable, has led and continues to lead to much confusion, as we shall see in some detail in the following chapter.

The ideal of communism is based primarily on Marx's view of man in capitalist society of the nineteenth century. For it is in terms of his analysis of man's condition in that period that he extrapolated to man's future ideal condition. His description of the ideal is largely negative, stating what conditions will not exist in communism.

We have seen that according to Marxism, man is the ensemble of his social relations. Man is defined collectively, because he is a collective being. Since each individual in society is defined by his collective essence, Marx further claims, he should enjoy his collective essence. He did so in the early primitive, collective societies. But in these societies men had only begun to realize their human potentialities. What man should become was and is to be decided in terms of what he could become, namely in terms of human potentiality, taken collectively. With the next stage of human development (viz. slave-holding society) at least some men were able to develop their potentialities to a much greater extent than previously.[23] Thus we have the emergence of the golden age of Greece. From this point of view Greek society was superior to primitive society.

But Greek society was a slave-holding society, and it as well as all ensuing class societies fell short or fall short of the ideal of man, because they are divided into classes, into haves and have-nots, into the dominated and the dominating. What is reprehensible in these societies is that man, a collective being, is divided against himself. The essence of man is still collective; he is still the ensemble of his social relations. But in a divided society, the individual man cannot express, experience, or enjoy his collective essence. His essence and existence are separated, and he in fact lives the life of a truncated individual man. Philosophers of such societies have traditionally sought the nature of man in the individual precisely because they found the individual separated and alone. For Marx, however, this condition of man was a distortion to be overcome.

According to Marxist theory, this division of man is the result of the division of labor, the fact that different individuals performed different tasks. In so acting, however, the individuals expressed themselves by increasingly selective activities and became increasingly truncated and one-sided. The division of man and his separation from other men was also brought about or was concomitant with the growth of private property. What one man had, separated him from others against whom he protected it. To the condition of man separated from man, Marx gives the name "alienation".[24] In capitalist society man is separated from other men, from the products of his labor (which belong to the entrepreneurs), and from his own productive activity (since he sells this in order to live). The alienation of man from man is seen most clearly in capitalist society, in which the capitalists exploit the workers and oppress them unmercifully. Marx's condemnation of the evils of capitalism is a moral condemnation in terms of what man can and should be. But capitalism also provides, according to Marx, the means whereby man may ultimately fulfill his potential and realize his ideal self. It provides the means necessary for man to dominate nature, to control his fate, and to produce the goods necessary for all men to have their needs satisfied. They can thus rise from the realm of necessity to the realm of freedom.[25]

For man to realize himself, to enjoy his control over nature, to have his needs satisfied, the conditions which produce man's alienation must be done away with, and man's alienation must be overcome. Man must be united to man, not separated from him; he must be allowed to share his common essence collectively. In order to achieve this, the Marxists assert, private property, which separates man from man, must be eliminated, and the division of labor must be done away with or at least so modified that each man will be capable of developing himself and harmoniously realizing his diverse capacities. The society in which there is no private property, no exploitation, no oppression, in which all men have their needs satisfied, in which each man is able to express himself and develop his capacities, and in which each individual can truly live his collective essence—such a society is by definition a communist society. This is the ideal in terms of which all societies and all men are judged, and in terms of which progress is measured.

The question which still remains unanswered, however, is how this ideal view is justified as a moral ideal, the only ultimate moral ideal of mankind. If communism is taken as a future state of mankind which will *inevitably* emerge, as some Marxists have held, then it ought not function as a moral ideal. For on this view each stage of man's development is necessary to produce the ultimate end, and each stage, including the last, is simply what it is. Each could not be otherwise, and so it is meaningless to judge any of them as if they could have been otherwise. The Soviet position, however, is not a fatalistic one, in which the end will unconditionally be achieved, no matter what. Rather communism is seen as an end which can be achieved, but which must be built. It will be achieved, therefore, only if certain positive actions are performed, only if the necessary means are taken.[26] If this is the case, then communism can serve as an ideal which should be realized, as a moral ideal. But its justification must lie not in its inevitability but elsewhere.

This justification has not been clearly worked out in the Marxist-Leninist literature. Value theory, with an analysis of what value is and how value judgments can be justified, is a little-developed discipline in the Soviet Union. But on the basis of what has appeared thus far,[27] values emerge when men evaluate phenomena, when they become objects of man's interest. Man can however, make erroneous evaluations, as when he thinks a certain object or action will lead to a certain desired end, though in fact it will not. Most objects and actions have value as means to ends. But are there some ends which are valuable in themselves? The answer which has emerged from the Soviet literature so far is that communism is the ultimate end which is good in itself. The reason it is good in itself, presumably, is because it is the condition of man in which he will be ultimately satisfied. Thus the satisfaction of man is the ultimate end; but the view of man envisaged is the collective view of man. What is good in itself is the satisfaction of man's desires, the fulfillment of his potentialities, not individually but collectively. The ultimate basis, then, is the collective nature of man and its fulfillment.

What is distinctive about the theory is that collective man, not individual man, is the source of value. This feature pervades all of Soviet ethical theory, and results in a systematic reinterpretation of key concepts such as "responsibility," "good," "happiness" and so on, to produce a view of morality which is quite distinct from the Western views most prevalent today.

We can now briefly recapitulate. Soviet ethics attempts to account for the origin and development of morality. It admits moral diversity, but attributes this to different physical and economic conditions in which societies find themselves. It admits a relative aspect of morality, but maintains that morality is ultimately objective, based on the needs of each society. It rejects any extrahuman source of morality and claims that morality grew out of the mores and customs of different societies. Yet it holds that the ends of any society can be evaluated against the ideal of mankind, communism. It defends this view by presenting an analysis of man as the aggregate of his social relations. That society is best which allows each man to develop his potentialities most fully and which enables each individual to enjoy his collective essence in harmony with his fellow men. The reason why this is best is ultimately because man is so constructed that this is what all men basically desire. The society in which man will become fully man and in which man's basic desires will be satisfied is by definition communistic. The achievement of communism is thus man's ultimate moral ideal and his criterion of morality.

This in sum is the basis of Soviet ethics. It is not an implausible theory. But its validity must be established. In order to do this we shall have to clarify a great many of the terms we have used, such as "alienation"; we shall have to examine the evidence given in support of factual claims; and we shall have to examine the logic of the whole process, including the claimed relation between fact and value. This, as well as an amplification of the content of the theory will occupy us for the two following chapters. In the remaining three chapters we will be concerned with the way this theory has been used in elaborating a communist moral code and the principles of communist morality, as well as with the implementation of this morality in Soviet society.

Chapter III

Good and the Moral Ideal

Since the appearance of G. E. Moore's *Principia Ethica* in 1903, the analysis of "good" has been one of the major concerns of Anglo-American moral philosophers although it has, by contrast, received comparatively little attention from Soviet philosophers, and in fact has scarcely been discussed until the last few years. But the communist moral ideal, the concrete embodiment of what is considered ultimately good or worthwhile, is central to Soviet ethics and represents the keystone of the system. Its meaning and justification must be carefully ascertained and examined, which task this chapter will attempt.

According to Soviet theory, "good" is one of several basic ethical categories. Ethical categories are the most general concepts of morality.[1] The most important of these are good, duty, conscience, honor, and happiness, though there is no unanimity about whether the list is complete or about precisely how one establishes which categories are basic. Some argue that more categories should be added to the list, while others have omitted some of those named. G. K. Gumnitskii, for instance, claims that justice and humaneness should be included and happiness dropped from the list of basic ethical categories;[2] A. F. Shishkin treats only duty, honor, conscience, and happiness in his widely used ethics text.[3] Various positions have been suggested in the periodical literature.[4] The predominant view, however, seems to be that good is not only one of the most fundamental but also the most general of the ethical categories. L. M. Arkhangel'-skii, who has written a basic work on the topic, calls the category of good the broadest of the ethical categories, embracing all the others and serving as their foundation.[5] As expressive of the most general positive moral evaluation, it is in fact identical to "moral."[6] On this interpretation "good" (in its ethical sense) means "moral" and "moral" means "good."

35

The Soviet approach to categoreal analysis is different from conceptual analysis as practiced in the British tradition. The Soviet approach is historical. The claim is that the meaning and content of categories change from era to era and from class to class. To determine the meaning of a term such as "good," therefore, it is necessary to see what the term meant historically. Such an investigation yields the historical components of the term. Similar components of the term in its historical meanings can be isolated by comparative analysis. Resulting is the concept's logical structure or form,[7] but its formal aspect is empty without its historical content. Part of the Soviet objection to Kant and to the positivists is that they are concerned only with formal analysis of concepts to the exclusion of historical content. For like reason they reject G. E. Moore's claim that "good" is indefinable and that any attempt to define it leads to committing the "naturalistic fallacy." For Moore's argument, they assert, is based on the false premise that "good" or any other term might be defined once and for all, as if it had some sort of eternal essence. Soviet philosophers would agree with Moore that any such attempt to define "good" would be impossible. However, this does not mean that "good" cannot be approached historically. The fact that men have historically called many different things good does not mean that "good" is not definable in terms of any of them, nor does it mean that what is good must ultimately be a matter of intuition. Rather, in order to elucidate the meaning of "good," it is the moral philosopher's job to discover precisely what was considered good in various stages of history and then to uncover the general common form of the category. Once this has been done categoreal analysis is completed by showing the relationship of the given category to other related ethical categories, since all the categories together are the conceptual apparatus used to reflect or describe that form of social consciousness which is called "morality."

In 1960 V. P. Tugarinov argued with a good deal of cogency that though "good" had many religious and idealistic overtones which are inimical to Marxism, Marxist philosophers could not for these reasons avoid analysis of this basic category if they wished their ethics to be a "strict and systematic theoretical science and not simply a collection of empirical rules of behavior,"[8] as it had in large part been up until then. According to him, good and evil are social concepts referring to social phenomena, or more precisely to human evaluations of these phenomena. "Good" is based on human goals and needs. The moral sense of "good" is bound up with morality as a social phenomena, and generally speaking, "good" as a moral concept equals "what is useful for society or for a certain class or group, what satisfies its needs and helps it achieve its goals."[9] What different societies or classes have considered good, of course, varies from society to society and from class to class. Gumnitskii adds to this that "immorality" (or evil) consists in the denial of the interests of the society or class or group in preference to one's own personal interests.[10]

This initial approach to "good" is based both on the general meaning of the term as referring to what is positively related to man so as to fulfill his needs or lead to his goals, and on the notion of morality as referring to the form of social consciousness concerned with those rules and norms which are necessary for social development.

The claim is that this approach is a descriptive, empirical approach to an analysis of "good." It is based on the empirical claim that societies do have needs and goals, and that they approve of actions which they believe will help them fulfill their needs or achieve their goals and disapprove of those which they believe will not. It is possible that their beliefs are mistaken. Therefore it is possible for someone to say that though society holds a certain action to be good, it is in fact evil. "Good" is not simply equivalent to what a society believes, but it also has an objective referent in society's actual needs and goals.

What if some individual holds that an action is good if it benefits him personally, though it harms his society? The Marxist-Leninist answer here is twofold. First, this approach, characteristic of an individualistic outlook, fails to appreciate the social origin and function of morality. Morality arises from the fact that man is a social being, that he is what he is because of society, and that as part of society his good is in general in-

ferior to the good of the whole, all other things being equal. But
he is also part of the whole. Consequently, if more good were done
to the individual than harm to society as a whole, presumably
more overall good to society would be achieved by an action
that benefited the individual. In this case the overall good of
society is still the ultimate criterion. If on the other hand more
harm were done to the society by a certain action than good
done to the individual, the action could not be called morally
good, except by adopting a special and not generally used meaning of the term. Such a new meaning of the term may be adopted,
but it would have nothing in common with the form of the
concept as it has been historically used.

Secondly, the Marxist-Leninist view maintains that an action, to be morally good, must be considered good not only by
the person performing it but also by anyone else in identical
circumstances. The individual is then properly considered as a
member of a class, for moral good refers to the fulfillment of the
interests of a class or of society. An exclusively individualistic
meaning of good is therefore a negation of morality because it
negates its social origin and function. The question of meaning
is here distinct from the question of how to decide between
conflicting claims concerning the moral worth of an action in a
class society when different classes have different and mutually
exclusive goals and needs.

Based on this initial approach to good the Marxist-Leninist
analysis goes on to examine the types of phenomena which are
called good. These include man himself, certain human qualities,
certain human motives, the results of human actions, and relations between men taken singularly or collectively.[11] The question of the specific content of good thus involves one in a study
of what individual classes held to be good, which character traits
they admired, which motives they considered honorable, which
actions they thought helped their society, all based on their differing aims and needs.

The extent to which those things considered good by different societies varies is an index of the class-content or relativity
of the content of the concept good. Those traits or actions which
are approved by all societies because they are necessary to the

functioning and development of every society make up the universal or all-human content of the concept good.[12]

This analysis of the meaning of "good," however, does not yet tell us how to decide between evaluations from different points of view by different classes of what is good. To stop here would be to remain neutral among disputing claims.

What is needed to decide between conflicting claims about a society's needs and goals is some moral criterion which has universal applicability and can be used as a measure or guide. For some Soviet philosophers this criterion is merely an aspect of good, derived from an analysis of the developing historical content of "good" up through the period of the development of socialist society. Regardless of whether it is derived from a study of the meaning of "good" or whether it is derived from the study of a larger context, Soviet philosophers are agreed that there is a criterion which expresses the highest good for man and which can be used for choosing among competing moral goals. The Soviet position thus involves a transition from an analysis of the meaning of "good" to a consideration of the nature of what is truly good for mankind. To clarify and evaluate the Soviet position we should: 1) examine their proposed criterion of morality, its content and justification, and 2) investigate the relation between fact and value according to the Soviet view, since good is moral value.

1) According to Soviet ethical theory the ultimate criterion of morality and the highest moral ideal is communism.[13] As a criterion of morality, it serves as a measure of what is moral or immoral. Whatever contributes towards the achievement of communism is moral; whatever hinders the achievement of communism is immoral. As a moral ideal it serves as a goal which is to be achieved. It is neither an illusion nor a utopia, but a realizable ideal connected with the actual development of contemporary society.[14]

The fact that communism is both the criterion of morality and a moral ideal is significant. As an ideal it is future oriented and is something *to be* realized or approached. It is distinct from present actuality.[15] As a criterion it carries these characteristics with it and serves as a double measure. On the one hand, any state of affairs which falls short of the ideal falls short of the criterion of morality and is to that extent imperfect. On the other hand the morality of any act can be judged not by whether it achieves the ideal, but by whether it tends to approach it. The criterion, therefore, does not as such state any absolute rules which are to be followed, though some general or more proximate rules of conduct might be, and in fact in Soviet ethics are, derived from it.

Now any moral criterion, if it is to fulfill its function, must be both meaningful and universally applicable. It must be meaningful for unless we understand what it means we will not be able to use it as a criterion of moral judgment. It must be universally applicable, where this means that it can be used in deciding in all cases whether any x (where x stands for whatever is a proper object of moral evaluation) is moral or immoral. The reason it must be universally applicable is that if it were not, then in those cases in which it were not applicable another criterion would have to be used (or these cases would fall outside the possibility of moral evaluation, making the first criterion universal in fact). But if another criterion is used then either both criteria can be derived from another more basic criterion or there would be a dual criterion. Both of these alternatives are rejected by the Soviet philosophers since they claim there is only one ultimate moral criterion, namely communism.

Let us first get clear the meaning of "communism" and examine its applicability as a criterion of moral judgment; we can then go on to an examination of the validity of the claim that communism is the moral ideal of mankind.

i) We have already seen Marx's embryonic formulation of communism as a future state of society. It is a state of society operating according to the formula "from each according to his ability, to each according to his need"; a society in which there is no oppression, no exploitation of man by man, and in which each man is given the opportunity to achieve his full, all-round development. Engels and Lenin did not significantly develop the meaning of communism further. The fullest statement or definition of communism is given in the Party Program of the Communist Party of the Soviet Union (1961):

Communism is a classless social system with one form of public ownership of the means of production and full social equality of all members of society; under it, the all-round development of people will be accompanied by the growth of the productive forces through continuous progress in science and technology; all the springs of cooperative wealth will flow more abundantly, and the great principle 'From each according to his ability, to each according to his needs' will be implemented. Communism is a highly organized society of free, socially conscious working people in which public self-government will be established, a society in which labor for the good of society will become the prime vital requirement of everyone, a necessity recognized by one and all, and the ability of each person will be employed to the greatest benefit of the people.[16]

In its essentials this definition adds little to Marx's notion of communism. But contemporary Soviet theoreticians, it is held, cannot specify in detail what communist society will be like because it is yet to be built.[17] Presumably the Party's general statement of communism is sufficient to guide social development at the present time, and more details about the actual running of the society will emerge as its realization draws nearer. If this is the case, then either all the essential ingredients of communism as a moral ideal are contained in the above definition or there are more to be added in time. If the latter is the case, then the same means by which the ideal of communism was arrived at in the first place should be continuously utilized to develop the ideal further. Thus, just as Marx saw the injustice of the conditions of the working man under capitalism and sought to achieve a society free from exploitation, so one could look for injustices in contemporary society or in some future state of socialist society and build the absence of those evils into the ideal of communism.

How does one know what is unjust? By what criterion does one judge? The answer evidently would be that one would judge by means of the criterion which had been previously formulated by the progressive elements of society, where by "progressive" is meant those who would inherit the future of the society. Capitalists were progressive with respect to feudalism; but in capitalist society the proletariat became the heirs of the future. Thus Marx used the morality of the proletariat to envisage what it needed, and he built this into his ideal of communism. This in turn will be developed and expanded, until all the needs of mankind are finally stated in their fullness in a complete statement of communism, which is the limiting case of the moral ideal. If this interpretation is accepted, then the content of the moral ideal is at present only partial, though its positive content will simply be augmented, not superseded. Thus "communism" is the name given to that future state of society which will have certain known characteristics $(e,f,g, . . .)$ as well as certain other characteristics $(m,n,o, . . .)$ which are yet to be determined. In accordance with the Party Program, presumably communism will be built "in the main" when $e,f,g, . . .$ are achieved, though this will not preclude its constant improvement.

According to another possible interpretation the essentials of communism consist only of those characteristics enumerated in the definition above: classless social system, one form of public ownership of the means of production, full social equality of all members of society, all round development of the people, and so on. Any society that achieves these characteristics will be communistic and will have achieved the moral ideal.

On either interpretation a task which still remains is the clarification of the various characteristics of communism and the consideration of whether they are such as can be achieved completely, or whether they admit of degrees. What constitutes a classless society? If "class" is to be used only in the sense of separating oppressors from the oppressed as seems to be the Marxist-Leninist interpretation[18] is it legitimate to speak of a "new class" in socialist society, as Djilas does? What does "full social equality of all members of society" mean, precisely and in detail? These and similar questions are questions the answers to which should ultimately be made precise if the composite moral ideal to which Soviet philosophers give the name "communism" is to be meaningful.

That the meaning of communism has not been fully elucidated is a fact. But this fact merely points to a task which is to be done. The ideal does not necessarily stand or fall because of the precision or imprecision, clarity or lack of clarity with which it has been stated. But the fact that the term is admittedly fuzzy does raise some question about its present applicability.

ii) To speak of communism as the criterion of morality, if the above analysis is correct, is somewhat misleading. For it is not a specific, usable measure. Rather it is the name of a complex state of society having certain characteristics, some of which are specified with varying degrees of precision, some of which are yet to be determined. As a present criterion only those characteristics which are part of its present content can be used for purposes of moral evaluation. Two problems emerge here with respect to the question of universal applicability.

The first concerns the attempt to use the criterion in difficult cases. Suppose we are faced with a choice between two acts, one of which seems to foster "the all-round development of the people" and the other of which seems to foster "full social equality" at the expense of all-round development. Each is an ingredient in the complex moral criterion which constitutes the content of communism. Which component is more important? How are we to decide in cases of conflict in the use of different components of the moral criterion?

So far there has been no Soviet discussion of this problem, and the criterion of communism is treated as if it were a simple unambiguous principle. Two answers seem possible. The first is that all the characteristics which make up communism are so closely bound together that any act which tends to realize one aspect automatically tends to realize the other, and that therefore no conflict of the type I have suggested is possible. Any such claim, however, if made, would have to be defended and seems *prima facie* implausible. The second possible reply would be to admit a possible conflict but to supply a second-order principle or rule which could be used to resolve such conflicts. Such a rule presumably would be or would be based on some characteristic of communism more fundamental than the two characteristics in conflict. Thus, for instance, some principle of social harmony or of the greatest possible harmonious blending of positive characteristics might be spelled out. Such a principle, if it were forthcoming, would also have to be defended and its derivation justified. But it might plausibly be treated either as one of the components of communism which has not yet been specified, or as a logically necessary regulative principle.

The second problem concerns the universality of the criterion's applicability. Let us suppose that the problems of what the criterion means and of how its components are to be reconciled have been satisfactorily solved. Can the criterion be effectively used in principle to solve all questions of moral evaluation? The Soviet reply here seems to be implicitly affirmative. On the basis of the moral criterion of communism Soviet philosophers claim to deduce certain moral principles which make up the moral code of the builders of communism, which we shall examine in Chapter V. These moral principles are the Soviet equivalent of the traditional Ten Commandments, and like the latter suffer from the defect of vagueness. They must be interpreted. If broadly enough interpreted, however, there is no reason to deny that they could, in principle, be used to solve all cases. That there are still disputes of interpretation and many admittedly unsolved questions does not necessarily affect the question of the universal applicability of the criterion in principle. However, a final judgment on this issue must await the prior clarifications mentioned above.

iii) If we grant the meaningfulness of the criterion of communism and its universal applicability we can go on to examine the claim that it is the moral ideal of mankind.

This claim can be interpreted in several ways. It might mean that all men have always implicitly held some (or many or all) of the characteristics which make up communism as their moral ideal. Or it might mean that the more progressive elements of society have held it as their moral ideal. Or it might mean that the most advanced elements of humanity today hold it as their ideal and that all mankind in some future time will hold it as its ideal. Each of these interpretations has some basis in Marxist theory, and in each instance a factual assertion is being made about what is held as a moral ideal by certain groups. But the Soviet claim goes further, holding not only that communism is the moral ideal of mankind, but that it is rightfully so, and that it is the highest or noblest or best or most perfect ideal that can or should be held. The first claim is one of fact. The second is a statement concerning value with an implied justification for the value judgment made.

The factual aspect of the claim requires empirical evidence to support it. If the first interpretation is followed, it would be maintained that all men have had as their moral ideal either all or at least some of the constituent parts of communism. To make such an assertion plausible it would have to be maintained that the identity in question is covert, that is, that men desired justice or equality and so on, though they did not necessarily use those terms. What they envisaged, however, was in some way the same or the embryonic beginning of what later became clearly formulated as the ideal of justice, equality, and the other components of communism. This claim could be defended if it could be shown that all men have always been so constructed psychologically either that they necessarily desired these conditions or implicitly saw them as ideals which should be fulfilled. This the Soviet philosophers have not yet done. Nor is it clear how they could since at least the ruling classes do not seem to have had equality as their ideal. Consequently, at best Soviet philosophers can hold that the component parts of communism were the ideal of the exploited masses. This claim could again be one of covert synonymity, and could be defended if it could be shown that oppression is inimical to the oppressed and leads to a desire for freedom from oppression and to the formulation of an implicit or explicit ideal of such freedom. A case might thus be made that some of the components of communism have been the ideal of significant portions of mankind, either explicitly or implicitly.

The stronger claims, however, that communism, as formulated for instance in the Party Program, is the moral ideal of mankind in the present, or that it will be the ideal of mankind in the future, are either not true or highly questionable. The ideals of a classless society and of the abolition of private ownership of the means of production, both components of communism in its present form, are obviously not the ideals of many people, especially of those living in "capitalist" countries. The assertion might become plausible if it were claimed, as some Soviet writers do claim, that it is the implicit ideal of *working mankind.*[19] But since a great many workers in capitalist countries seem to defend their own social system explicitly against the possibility of communism, such a claim involves the dubious assertion that somehow the Soviet writers know the real, though implicit, ideal of these workers better than the workers themselves. And Soviet writers have not shown why their assertions should be believed in this instance.

Little need be said about the claim that the communist moral ideal will be the ideal of all men in the future, for such a claim could be verified only in the future, and cannot be verified at the present time. It is a proposition which may well be believed, and presumably is believed by Soviet communists, although belief should not be confused with fact.

According to Soviet theory, the leaders of society have always preached that morality which benefited their interests, and have attempted to inculcate it in the people as a whole. It seems clear that the communist moral ideal is the ideal preached by the leaders of the Soviet Union, and it may be the actual ideal of many communists and noncommunists within and without the Soviet Union. But the question of how many people hold the communist moral ideal in its explicit Soviet formulation as their own is an empirical one about which, to my knowledge, there is no explicit empirical information. What Soviet writers do cite are figures about the millions of workers engaged in the struggle for communism.[20] But there is no reason to accept any simple equation between all the citizens of countries whose governments are run by communist parties and those who supposedly hold communism as their moral ideal.

The move from the question of whether the communist moral ideal is held in fact to that of whether it should be held is a move from fact to theory. The Soviet position is that the communist moral ideal is the highest moral ideal mankind has ever known and that it should be universally held. A consideration of the grounds for this assertion leads us to the Soviet view of the relation between facts and values, and to some of the facets of Soviet value theory in general.

2) We have seen that according to Soviet theory values emerge in the world only with man. A world devoid of con-

sciousness would also be devoid of value,[21] for values arises as a result of man's interests and needs. What satisfies his needs or becomes the object of his interest takes on value for the individual and as such is at least subjectively valuable. In addition some objects or actions, whether actually the object of interest or not, are necessary in order to achieve certain aims or goals, and these actions or objects take on value as means to achieve an end.

The relation of values to facts is a relation that exists through the intermediary of man. Man, who is always a social being and always in a social context, sees, grasps, reflects, or comes to know facts. But his approach to facts is most frequently from a point of view—the point of view of how they relate to or affect himself and his society. People from different societies and from different classes each assimilate facts into their own perspective, see them from their own point of view, or fit them into their own worldview. Thus, according to the Soviet view, truth and value are not two separate domains.[22] They are necessarily intertwined and intermixed. This presumably means that in actuality fact and value are always found together, and perhaps also that what counts as a fact may sometimes be related to one's point of view. Whether Soviet theory holds that fact and value cannot even be conceptually distinguished is not entirely clear. Yet on one point Soviet moral philosophers agree: the statement "Communism is mankind's highest moral ideal and greatest good" is, they claim, objectively true.

According to the Marxist-Leninist view, moral values are essentially social in origin. They are not the result of individual subjective interests or goals, but of the interests or goals of society as a whole. What is morally valuable is what helps the society function and progress. This is independent of the will of any particular individual or individuals, and in this sense moral values are objective. In a class society class interests and needs form the basis of moral values. But since these interests and needs are the result of the conditions in which the class finds itself, the moral values based on them are objective. Since the aims of different societies differ, as do the aims of different classes within a class society, moral evaluations may differ. Such differences, however, do not negate the objectivity of opposing moral evaluations. For objectivity is always relative to aims, interests, needs, and the actual conditions of society. Similarities of interest and aims lead to similarities in moral judgments. The core of these form the simple all-human values common to all societies.

The aims of differing societies and of different classes—and consequently their moral values—can themselves be judged by reference to the highest moral ideal, which, according to Marxism-Leninism, is communism. How can communism be defended as the highest moral ideal? The Soviet answer is that it is the only moral ideal that is truly basic or ultimate in the sense that it truly expresses the actual needs and interests of mankind. This answer deserves careful scrutiny.

The foundation for the Soviet claim is the Marxist view of man and of society. We have seen that man, according to Marx, Engels and the Soviet philosophers, is a social being whose essence is the ensemble of his social relations. The interests of man as man, therefore, cannot be expressed by the interests of any particular part of society at the expense of another part. For this would obviously be to express the interests of only a part of man. The moral ideals of any oppressor class, therefore, by their very nature cannot hope to express the interests of all mankind. The interests of the oppressed, however, *can* express the interests of all mankind. Since they are not oppressors their interests are not of such a nature that they can only be satisfied at the expense of some other group. The interests of the proletariat, the oppressed class under capitalism, are in fact the interests which are taken over into the ideal of communism.

Since Marxism holds that man can only be man when all men can share in their common essence, man can only be man in a classless society where there is no group that dominates another. This is basic. To it are added other interests and needs of man which are generally admitted to be universal: the desire for happiness, the need for food, drink, clothing, housing and the other necessities of life; the opportunity to develop one's abilities; the desire to be free from oppression. But all these take on new meaning in a classless society in which man is really man.

Happiness, for instance, has been cited as the end of man and his highest moral ideal at least from the time of Aristotle. But happiness for Aristotle and for all other spokesmen of a class society has always meant the happiness of the individual or of a select group. The Marxist-Leninists claim that the happiness of which utilitarians such as Mill speak is the happiness of individuals in a laissez-faire society, in a society of dog eat dog in which the spoils belong to the victor. It is the happiness of some men at the expense of others; and in a class society it is necessarily at the expense of others, for only the members of the exploiting class have the material means necessary to satisfy their wants and the opportunities necessary to pursue their happiness. Such happiness may be the goal of individual man. But if it is the moral ideal of society it can represent only a portion of that society. Happiness, the moral ideal of mankind, is not to be achieved at the expense of others. Rather, the happiness of each man is a necessary condition for the happiness of all men. According to Marxist theory, therefore, happiness as a moral ideal must be approached not only from the viewpoint of the individual but from the viewpoint of man as such or from the viewpoint of a classless society.

Three different aspects of happiness must be considered.[23] First of all, happiness requires the satisfaction of certain physical and psychological needs: material goods, appropriate social-political conditions (equality, freedom, justice), and cultural riches must be available to man.[24] One must have enough to eat and wear, a certain sense of security about his future, and the like. A communist society which operates according to the principle "from each according to his ability, to each according to his need," provides these objective conditions of happiness for all men, not just for a few. Secondly, each member of society must have the ability to make use of society's objective conditions in order to achieve happiness. Society must make these conditions equally available to all. This is as much as society can provide. On this basis the final achievement of personal happiness which is the final goal of each man, can be sought by each man, not all of whom may achieve the same degree of personal happiness. However, at least no man will achieve his happiness at the expense of another; the happiness of all men hence becomes a real possibility. Man is not an isolated individual but rather is a social being. The communist ideal of happiness is thus the expression of all men's ideal of happiness.

Now this view has a certain strength and appeal. If the communist moral ideal is indeed the embodiment of what the vast majority of men seem to have wanted through the centuries, namely happiness, freedom to express themselves, universal justice, material plenty, etc., and if part of this ideal is that these goods or values should be enjoyed by all men and not merely by some at the expense of the rest, then there seems to be reason for claiming that this is a higher ideal than one in which these qualities are to be enjoyed only by the few. Of course, most moral ideals have championed the universal satisfaction of man's needs and wants and the fulfillment of his basic desires. The Marxists recognize this, but assert that a communist society is the only one in which these values can actually be achieved by all since it is the only society without an oppressing class of rulers.

Now four different questions arise here: 1) Is the communist moral ideal actually an accurate statement of what men, because of their physical or psychological make-up, have always desired? 2) Is a classless society the only way in which these all-human values can best be achieved? 3) What is the relation of the means taken by a society to achieve these ends with respect to the ends themselves? 4) Is there any society emerging such that it gives hope of achieving the moral ideal of mankind?

1) The first question concerns the actual formulation of the content of communism as, for instance, in the Party Program. Is this a statement of the *highest* aspirations of mankind? It is not quite clear how to go about answering this question. One can legitimately wonder whether mankind has any common set of aspirations. Men's aims have been and remain diverse. Although it is possible to speak of the aims or aspirations of individuals or of groups and to learn of these either through their actions or statements, this is not true of mankind as such. One may claim to speak for all men, but any such claim is necessarily presumptuous and without an adequate empirical base.

The Party Program's formulation of communism contains a certain set of characteristics, possibly open to future additions, which Marxist-Leninists claim express man's highest aspirations. Now suppose we admit that many of its constituent parts such as freedom from oppression and satisfaction of needs are among the desires of man which seem to have accompanied him throughout his history. We may still question whether all the constituent parts listed *deserve* to be included, for instance public ownership of the means of production, and whether some characteristics which ought to have been included have been left out, for instance freedom of religious worship according to one's conscience. The latter is certainly something the oppressed masses have fought for in the past, despite the Marxist claim that religion is the instrument of the ruling classes. Since some people claim that religious worship is and has been a basic human need, and can defend this claim at least as well as Marxists can defend some of the components of communism, its absence from the highest human moral ideal may well be questioned. Contrariwise the public ownership of the means of production is a fairly recent concept and cannot be called one of man's basic human needs. The Soviet line, of course, is that this is a necessary means to achieve the absence of exploitation of man by man. But whether this is the case is disputed. Marx's analysis of capitalism and his labor theory of value were challenged soon after they appeared and have been convincingly challenged since.[25]

Whether the condition of the masses or of the working man is better or his standard of living higher in contemporary "capitalist" or contemporary socialist countries is hardly debatable, and the evidence clearly favors the "capitalist" worker. Whether state ownership of the means of production guarantees the worker less exploitation than private ownership does is perhaps a debatable matter, though contemporary history indicates a negative answer.

Our conclusion, therefore, can only be that even if it is possible to speak meaningfully of the aims and aspirations of mankind, the Soviet statement of what communism will be is not an adequate summary of them.

2) If we were once to agree on certain components of the highest moral ideal, we could next ask whether they could be enjoyed only in a classless society, as Marxism-Leninism maintains. The meaning and basis of a classless society are the issues here.

In Marx's view the division of society into classes meant that, as a result of the division of labor, one class must oppress the other. The division of society into classes led to a breach in the human essence, a division among men to which he gave the term "alienation," a term used somewhat differently before him by Feuerbach and Hegel.

Suppose we grant that a society in which there is no exploitation of man by man is, all other things being equal, more in accord with the moral ideal of mankind than one in which such exploitation exists; and that, again all other things being equal, a society with less oppression is more in accord with the moral ideal of mankind than one with a greater amount of oppression. We must still decide whether a given class society has more or less oppression and exploitation in it than a given classless society. Marx and his followers seem to claim almost by definition that a classless society has less oppression and exploitation than a class society. But using "class" in the Marxist-Leninist sense, one could well argue that there was more oppression of man by man in Stalin's Russia than there was in the United States during the same years.

Marx thought that by doing away with private property and with classes one did away with alienation, the division of labor, exploitation, and oppression. This was a gross oversimplification. In fact, the question of whether the division of labor can or should be done away with in a technological society has fairly recently and inconclusively been debated in the Soviet philosophical literature.[26] It has certainly not been eliminated in the Soviet Union though that country claims to have a classless society. Alienation, as used by Marx, was an economic as well as a moral category. Since private ownership of the means of production has been done away with, the Soviets claim that alienation of the type referred to by Marx has also been eliminated.[27] But even if this doubtful claim is accepted the question of whether the human essence might not have become fragmented in ways which Marx was unable to foresee is not settled. Critics in Eastern and Western Europe as well as in the United States claim with some cogency that alienation (in varying meanings of the term) continues in the Soviet Union despite the supposed absence of classes.[28]

Classlessness, according to Marxism-Leninism, is a sine qua non of the ideal moral society. But it seems rather that the absence of classes should be treated as one *possible* component of the moral ideal. If it is necessary in order to achieve the end of human exploitation, then it belongs to this ideal. But if it is not necessary, and if it possibly introduces more negative than positive moral value into the whole, then it does not belong. In any event it deserves constant reevaluation as a means and not automatic inclusion as an end.

3) Given the moral ideal of mankind, what means may morally be taken to achieve it? The Soviet answer is that whatever means are necessary in order to achieve the end are ipso facto moral. But this answer in fact begs the question. For the question is how does one decide which means are *necessary*, as opposed to being merely *expedient*. Some, for instance, have claimed that the improvement of the lot of the working man and the achievement of the Marxist ideal could be attained more effectively and morally by using the existing legal means available in capitalist countries rather than by employing violence and fomenting revolution. Ethical socialism sought the achievement of social justice before the advance of material production, and its adherents criticized Marxism for putting the latter before the former. With respect to the achievement of communism, the Marxist-Leninist position asserts that while those means which demoralize the masses or weaken their struggle would not be moral, the oppression or suppression of the enemies of communism by any means is moral.[29] But such a position justifies present oppression of a portion of mankind in the name of some future desirable state of another portion of mankind. While lack of oppression is the future ideal, this very ideal is used to justify present oppression. While the ideal is supposedly desired by all and to be enjoyed by all, it is used

against and at the expense of a certain group of men. The reply that only exploiters are to be oppressed is beside the point; for they too are members of mankind. The communist ideal is one of the future; in the hands of its Soviet champions it entails no present moral principles or rules. Anything and everything can be justified in the name of necessity, and necessity is determined by the leaders of the Party. The lack of present principles, if not a negation of the future ideal, in fact leaves, with respect to the enemies of communism, a moral void which can be used to justify any action, no matter how outrageous.

4) Whether there is a society which is progressing towards the achievement of the all-human moral ideal, and which society it is, are debatable and to a large extent empirical questions beyond the scope of this chapter or book. The fact that a country calls itself socialistic or communistic does not necessarily mean either that it embodies or is approaching even those ideals contained in the Party Program's description of communism, though presumably it is at least nominally striving for communism of some sort. The claim by Soviet philosophers that the Soviet Union is the true champion of the universal human moral ideal does not follow from the fact that the Soviet Union claims to be in the stage of building communism. One should carefully distinguish between the components of a moral ideal and the name "communism," lest in claiming to have achieved communism a society may either think or lead others to think that it has attained mankind's supposed moral ideal as well.

The upshot of our analysis is that the Marxist-Leninist treatment of good is at present far from complete. The Soviet historical-logical approach to categoreal analysis promises more than its Soviet practitioners deliver since, in fact, it is largely superseded by Soviet claims about the real nature of good. Though good, as all values, is relative to class interests and varies with them, the highest good, which is the highest moral value and the criterion of morality, is said to be communism, supposedly embodying the moral aspirations of all humanity. Upon analysis, however, we see that the meaning of "communism" is still extremely vague and ambiguous, that its universal application is therefore at best difficult, and that it cannot be shown actually to embody either all or most of what might loosely be called the aims and aspirations of mankind. Neither is it desired by all men, nor can it be shown that it should be.

As a convincing philosophical presentation of the moral meaning of "good," the Soviet position is seriously wanting. But as a statement of an ideal which can and has inspired men, communism can hardly be ignored. If communism is not the moral aim of all men, its achievement is the moral aim of many. If it is not, or cannot be shown to be, the highest human moral ideal, it has historically won the allegiance of too many to be lightly tossed aside. The practical implementation of the ideal of communism in the Soviet moral code will occupy us later in this work. A final aspect of the Marxist-Leninist development of "good," namely its relation to "duty," will be part of our concern in the following chapter.

Chapter IV

Freedom, Duty, and Moral Evaluation

Marxism is widely known as a deterministic theory. Determinism permeates it on many levels and in a variety of ways. Yet Soviet moral philosophers claim, together with a large number of non-Marxist philosophers, that man bears responsibility for certain actions he performs and that he cannot be responsible unless he is in some sense free. The initial concern of this chapter, therefore, will be to unravel the tangled threads of freedom and determinism which are woven into the Marxist-Leninist ethical position, and to clarify the meaning of such terms as "freedom," "responsibility," "duty," and "conscience," all of which enter into Soviet discussions of evaluations made from the moral point of view.

The Soviet position starts from the postulate of universal causality, which is roughly formulated as holding that "there is a necessary relation among phenomena such that one necessarily produces the other."[1] "Determinism" is defined as a theory which acknowledges the objective existence of causal laws which extend to all phenomena.[2] Any form of indeterminism which denies the existence and efficacy of causal laws is thus rejected at the outset, as is any sense of "freedom" which involves or implies indeterminism. The Soviet position is neither mechanistic nor fatalistic, and Soviet philosophers explicitly dissociate it from such views, which they attribute to Laplace and pre-Marxist materialists. Fatalism is the view that whatever happens happens necessarily and will happen no matter whether or not, or how, action is taken. This view is rejected because it denies the efficacy of human action. The Laplacian view claims that if one knew the position and momentum of all the particles in nature at any given moment, and the mechanical laws governing their movement, he could know their position at any past or future moment. Thus the future is completely contained in the past, and what-

57

ever happens happens necessarily and inevitably. Human choice is therefore an illusion, since all choice is completely determined. The establishment of the uncertainty relation in quantum mechanics precludes our knowing exactly both the position and the momentum of individual microparticles, consequently precluding the full realization of the Laplacian ideal of knowledge. However, the question of whether there are laws which we can never learn governing individual microparticles and the question of whether in any sense one could have chosen otherwise than the way one did in fact choose are both left open.

Marxism-Leninism rejects mechanistic determinism because it claims that in reality there are a multitude of forms of causal connection, not all of which can be reduced to mechanistic causality.[3] Thus economic laws are not reducible to laws of physics and could not be expressed in physicalist terms. This does not mean that economic depressions do not have causes, but that the type of causality operative in economics is different from that which operates upon physical bodies. The Soviet position maintains that with the introduction of man and reasoned choice, a kind of nonmechanistic causality becomes operative which cannot be handled in mechanistic terms.[4]

For the purposes of ethics we should distinguish four mutually related levels of causality in terms of which the Marxist-Leninist position can be most favorably interpreted. These are the properly material or the realm of physical nature; the economic; the superstructural, and especially the moral; and the individual.

Nature is governed by causal laws. These laws operate with necessity, and certain physical conditions prevail at certain times in the history of the universe in general and of the earth in particular. Although the laws of nature apply universally, this type of causation does not preclude other types which operate within the framework of the laws of nature. With the appearance of man and society a new order of causality is introduced into the world. Man not only reacts, but can choose among various reactions. He can learn the laws of nature and utilize them to achieve his own ends.

Three claims are involved here in the Marxist-Leninist position. First, it is because nature is determined that man can learn the laws of its operation and utilize these laws to achieve his ends. Secondly, society, which is the aggregate of men in their mutual interrelations, is different in kind and activity from other bodies or aggregates. The laws which govern its operation and development are not reducible to physical laws because the categories used to describe society are not expressible in the categories of the natural sciences. "Slave," "master," "private property" and like terms are not expressible in terms of the position or state of physical particles. For the Soviets such nonreducibility is the result of a dialectical leap. Thirdly, though the activities of man are limited by physical laws and by his physical environment, within these limits he can utilize the physical laws to modify his environment. Thus we can say that the laws of nature and physical geographic conditions of a given society remain essentially the same over long periods of time and set limits to what that society can do. But within these limits, as society learns and utilizes the laws of nature, it can change considerably. The physical geography of what we call the Soviet Union has changed little since 1300, yet its society has changed significantly. The limits of what it could achieve at any point in its development is determined by its setting and the laws of nature. But these alone are insufficient by themselves to explain the actual development of Soviet society.

Thus far there is little novel in the Soviet position. The claimed nonreducibility of social laws to physical laws is not unique to Marxism-Leninism, and the claimed dialectical leap which separates these two orders adds nothing to the claim of nonreducibility. Soviet discussions throw no light on the question of whether the irreducibility of social to physical categories is simply a result of man's linguistic poverty. The question as to whether two different descriptions of the same event, one in terms of social relations and final causes, and the other in terms of physical states and mechanical causes, might with additional knowledge be equally valid is at this point left open.

Economic determinism, however, is a particular type of social determination strongly emphasized by Marx and taken over by his Soviet followers. Exactly what the contemporary

Soviet position on economic determinism is, is by no means easy to ferret out. Although the language which Soviet philosophers use is that of Marx, they have softened Marx's claims to such a large extent that the import of the doctrine of economic determinism is no longer clear.

Just as the laws of nature and the physical environment determine the possibilities open to a society, so Marxism-Leninism claims that within any society its economic conditions determine its development and the life of its members. The force of "determine" here is of central importance to the Marxist-Leninist position, and it seems to come closest to "limit" or "set a limit to the possibilities of" on the one hand, and to "provide impetus and opportunities for" on the other. Though what a society is capable of doing is limited by its economic conditions, its economic conditions also impel the society along certain lines of development. To speak of the "necessary character of social development" is for Soviet philosophers to speak of its general tendency.[5]

The more specific Marxist-Leninist claim with which we are concerned is the claim that the economic conditions of society determine the morality of that society. If we follow through the above interpretation, this presumably means that economic conditions set limits to the possible moralities which can be adopted by a society. Only in a society which recognizes private property can stealing become immoral. Moreover, presumably those actions which tend to promote the development of the society are judged by the society to be moral, and those which are harmful are judged to be immoral.

If the Soviet claim is that the economic conditions of a society are merely one important factor in determining a society's morality, it would scarcely be a claim unique to Marxism-Leninism. Marxist-Leninists, however, claim much more. They claim that economic conditions are the one ultimately determining factor both in a society's morality and in the ethical theories which that society produces.

But their claim is considerably mitigated by their concomitant admission of the "relative independence" of morality and ethics. Soviet philosophers admit that from knowledge of the economic conditions of a society one cannot deduce its morality. First, a variety of different actions might be compatible with the development of a society, and which of these a society hits upon depends on factors other than its economic base. Secondly, the morality of any society at any given time is influenced by its historically antecedent morality, by the customs which are carried over with or without modification from previous generations and by its past and present politics, religion, philosophy, education, etc.[6] Thirdly, the society may be mistaken as to what will advance or retard its development, and so may prescribe for its members what in fact it should not. These three conditions tend to take the sting out of the claimed determination of morality by economic conditions. It becomes sufficiently vague and open to exception so that it cannot be shown to be either a false or a true claim with any amount of rigor. For in any given instance, if the base changes and there is no resulting change in the morality of a society this can be attributed to the lag of consciousness behind being. This is the Soviet explanation for the continuance of Christian morality from feudal times through the present in many societies. It seems likely that changing economic conditions are accompanied by changes in morality; but when Soviet philosophers admit that law, education, and politics can also change morality, and that changes in all of these and in morality may also affect the economic conditions of a society—as the doctrine of the active influence of the base according to Marxism-Leninism seems to imply[7]—then the distinctiveness of the Soviet claims of economic determinism disappears.

The Soviet reply would no doubt be that although other forces besides economic ones influence morality and ethics, in the final analysis these forces are themselves determined by the economic conditions of society. What could this mean? Let e stand for economic forces, and $l, m, n, \ldots$ for law, morality, religion, etc. The claim might mean that e sets the limits within which $l, m, n \ldots$ can develop, but not vice-versa. This claim, however, is false. For there are many instances in which law or religion set limits to economic development. One need think only of the regulation of big business by law in the United

States and the effect of certain religious beliefs in India on the economic development of that country. We have already seen that the claim cannot be that e influences $l, m, n, \ldots$ but that these do not influence e, for the latter influence is specifically admitted by Soviet philosophers. Other interpretations might be possible, though none have been explicitly given by the Marxist-Leninists. When we consider further that the economic realm is not a distinct realm at all but is intertwined at least in relatively advanced societies with law and politics, we see that no clear meaning can be given to the claim. It seems simply to be a vacuous reiteration of a strong claim of economic determinism which stands in contradiction to the admitted influences and counterinfluences of the superstructure.

Marx's position on economic determinism involved a confusion between what he called the "material life" of society and the economic forces of that society. Denying idealism, he claimed that matter was basic and spirit secondary. But he brought this metaphysical claim into the life of man in the form of the base-superstructure model, overlooking the fact that the economic structure of society is not material in any metaphysical or ontological sense. He also claimed that classes and class interests were determined by economic considerations only or primarily, ignoring such other real drives as love, sex, religious belief, and the desire for power. Contemporary Soviet philosophers seem to wish to correct Marx's overstatements but to keep his basic claim—a task which they have not been able to accomplish.

Any strong claim of economic determinism would undermine the Soviet position as it has developed. With respect to ethics, if all ethical views are determined by economic conditions, then the Marxist and Soviet positions are determined by them as well as the bourgeois positions. The fact that Emperor Marcus Aurelius and Epictetus the slave each held almost identical stoic doctrines shows that ethical views are not determined only by a philosopher's class position or economic interests. If Marxist-Leninist ethics represents the views of the masses or of the future classless generations, this would show it was a popular theory, but not necessarily a correct one. Marxist-Leninist *ethical theory,* moreover, is held and preached by philosophers, not by the masses; and it can be shown that in this area Soviet philosophers have been completely subservient to the needs and demands of the Communist Party.[8] If Soviet ethics does present the only correct view of morality, it must stand on its own feet and show that it accounts for morality better than any other view.

With respect to morality, a strong claim of economic determinism would similarly undermine the Soviet position. If what a class holds to be good is determined solely by its economic position, then what the classless society holds to be good is similarly determined. But if this were the case, then there would be no moral reason for holding that what the classless society says is good is to be preferred to what any particular class says is good. We have seen, however, that the Marxist-Leninist position involves a dual view of what is good. In one sense good is relative to class interests and circumstances; but these competing goods can themselves be judged with respect to a more ultimate good based on the true collective nature of man. Although economic determinism accounts for the relative nature of good, it makes impossible an explanation or defense of the ultimate good in terms of which the relative goods are judged by Marxist-Leninists. Soviet philosophers are thus faced with a dilemma. If economic conditions and interests always determine what is held to be good, then they cannot defend the existence of an ultimate good which they call communism and which is supposed to be good independent of economic considerations. But if they admit that an ultimate good can be defended independent of present economic conditions, they in fact give up economic determinism in any strong sense. Their attempts to explain their own meaning of "good" in terms of universal human aspirations but all other meanings of "good" in terms of economic considerations is a reflection of their unwillingness to face the dilemma. Soviet philosophers, therefore, either do not or should not hold a strong form of economic determinism. Although economic factors influence and help circumscribe human possibilities, they are one of a number of factors which mutually interact and which concomitantly affect human action.

The Soviet view of economic determinism, whether held in a strong or weak form, pertains only to classes or large groups.

The final level in the Soviet presentation of determinism is the individual level. The laws of nature and the environment set limits and provide limited possibilities for the development of the economy of a society. This sets limits and provides opportunities for the development of the superstructure and in particular the morality of a society. This in its turn provides limits for the activity and development of the individuals in a society. Men are born into and grow up in a society with certain possibilities open to them and with certain demands made upon them. Within the limits set by their society they may act one way or another, and choose one way or another. However, no given individual is completely determined by nature, by the economic base of his society, or by its morality to make one choice instead of another. Nature, economic conditions, and morality limit his possible actions and tend to push him in certain ways, but all these causal factors must go through the filter of the acting individual, whose individual reaction to the exterior causal stimuli is not always predictable.

In sum, if we consider physical nature, the economic base of society, the morality of that society, and an individual within that society we can distinguish within the Soviet position four levels of causality. Each more exclusive or higher level of causality depends upon the more inclusive or lower level or levels in that its causality operates within limits established by it (or them). Within the various levels man can utilize the laws of its operation in order to achieve his own ends, chosen from among those made available to him by each successive level. By making certain decisions or choices among mutually exclusive possibilities in the higher levels man can modify the lower levels to some extent, though always in accordance with the laws governing those lower levels.

It is on the basis of this understanding of determinism or causal determination that the Marxist-Leninists approach the question of freedom.[9] As we have seen they reject any meaning of "freedom" which involves indeterminism or an uncaused event, be it a choice or an action. Freedom is to be defined within the deterministic framework. It arises not in the world of objects but in the world of men. Freedom, which is never absolute or complete, but always relative to a number of factors, is predicable only of a conscious, knowing, goal-oriented, active being or group.[10] A proper analysis of human freedom, moreover, is not to be sought in an examination of man as a separate being or individual, but of man as he really is in his social context. The Marxist-Leninist conception of human freedom, as of human nature itself, is not individual but always collective.

Man's freedom depends on his ability to reflect and to learn to utilize the laws of nature and of social development. In any given society men are free to the extent that they realize the possibilities which are open to them, that they choose among those possibilities, and that they employ their knowledge of the laws of nature or of social development in order to achieve their aims. The more capable they are of achieving such aims, the more free they are. Freedom is thus a function of knowledge, choice, and efficacious action, each of which is taken primarily in a social and secondarily in an individual sense, and each of which, according to Marxist-Leninists, involves "insight into necessity."

The first prerequisite of freedom is knowledge. One must have knowledge of the way nature and society are determined. The more man knows about the laws of nature the more he can utilize them. In this sense man is free to make synthetic fabrics, light up his homes and streets, and increase his crop yield by using his knowledge of natural laws, and by his insight into the causal relations existing in the natural order. In like manner, using economic laws he can help avert depressions and crises and help guide the development of society. However, the knowledge to which we refer is acquired by men collectively; it is an aggregate of individual contributions. Knowledge is socially acquired, socially transmitted, and socially utilized. In this sense man through time has become more and more free, more and more the master of nature and to some extent of society.

Secondly, knowledge is a function of choice, which here does not mean arbitrary whim. Man is free only to the extent that he sees the real choices offered to him by the situation in which he finds himself, by the physical and economic conditions in which he lives. Man may choose to do the impossible; but this is a vacuous choice, ineffective, and not properly termed free, since it cannot lead to the attainment of the chosen end. Man is only free when he sees within his determined limits what can be chosen—and so again this is a kind of insight into necessity. Necessity here is not inevitability but the delimitation of possibilities.[11] To equate necessity with inevitability would be to say that only what will be chosen was possible, and that nothing else could have been chosen. This would be to deny the efficacy of choice, which the Soviet philosophers do not do.[12] To the extent that goals chosen are social goals and the ends social ends, freedom is social and not individual.

Lastly, men must not only know what can be done and choose among these possibilities, but their freedom consists in actually acting on their choice, employing the means they have chosen, and achieving their ends. Where, as above, the ends sought were social ends, the action is similarly social—the production of goods, the prevention of economic crises, the development of society, all of which are achieved only by social activity, based on insight into the necessary means which must be used to achieve the desired ends.

The freedom of man which we have discussed thus far is the freedom of collective man, the growing freedom of man in dominating nature and directing society.

In the Soviet view social freedom is the necessary prerequisite for individual freedom.[13] The prerequisites for the effective exercise of individual freedom are initially similar to those necessary for the exercise of social freedom. A man is free when he chooses a real possibility based on his knowledge of the circumstances and regularities involved and takes the action necessary to achieve his chosen goal. His choices are, however, more restricted than are those of society. For society as such has more knowledge than any individual, and can collectively do much that an individual cannot do. The individual is free to the extent that he can share in the knowledge of society and to the extent that he can actually utilize this knowledge to achieve his goals. Part of man's freedom consists in his taking part in the freedom of society, developing productive forces, improving social relations, and acquiring and disseminating knowledge.[14]

The exercise of personal freedom depends in addition on having the opportunity to achieve his goal and on having an absence of external constraint.

It is in the latter sense that the problem of freedom has been most dealt with in Western philosophy, where political freedom is generally associated with lack of constraint on personal activity by the government, and where individual freedom is based on the ability to make choices without any external physical or psychological determining force. While Soviet philosophers admit these aspects of freedom they emphasize first that to stop with these considerations is to consider only freedom of choice or freedom in a capitalist society for those who have the necessary money to do what they want. Freedom of all men in society necessitates not only eliminating constraints where possible, but also supplying positive opportunities for all actually to exercise their choice and to take the actions necessary to realize their aims. The proletariat, chained to their machines and having barely enough to subsist on, can scarcely be said to have had freedom of travel or of the press or of choice of occupation since they had no opportunities to exercise the freedom which was supposedly guaranteed them by law. Secondly, to consider only lack of constraint and not positive opportunity is to abstract an individual from his society, and to speak of an empty freedom of choice without considering real freedom of action.

With respect to the question of freedom and the psychological determination of the individual, the Soviet position resembles what is known as soft-determinism. Freedom involves the absence of external restraint and the ability to choose among alternatives. In the process of choice both external and internal factors influence a person's decisions. He is a product of his society and is influenced by it; he also brings with him his own physical constitution, impulses, memory, education and past—all of which play a part in his choice or decision. But a choice or a decision cannot be the result simply of a tug of war between conflicting motives; otherwise the motives would decide his choice or make his decision independent of him, and he would be a passive spectator who then for some unknown reason falsely believes that he has chosen or decided.[15] The psychological basis of freedom is the ability of a man to react to stimuli electively, to evaluate possible variants with the help of reason, and to decide among or between them for known reasons.[16]

This is as far as the Soviet analysis of individual freedom has gone. The question of how the individual decides, if it is not merely a question of the strongest motive winning out, is not answered. While it is admitted that several lines of determinism—internal and external—are operative, it is not clear what determines which choice is made or which line is to dominate. A. P. Chermenina suggests that the subject is the author of a new, unpremeditated line of determination,[17] and that his resulting action, as unpredictable, is truly creative.[18] Whether this means simply that a particular individual's makeup is so complex that neither the individual details nor the laws governing his actions are or can be known in sufficient detail to predict his particular actions, or whether it means more than this is not clear. The study of the individual psychology of morality still awaits its development in the Soviet Union. In classical Marxism the masses made history and their motives, to the extent that they led to historically significant action, were determined by the economic conditions of society. But now that the individual has appeared in the Marxist-Leninist scheme, the extent to which at least some of his actions are not completely specified by his socioeconomic conditions requires a yet-awaited clarification of such terms as "motive," "intention," and "will" on the individual level.

The position that people do really decide and make choices is in accord with common sense and is held by many non-Marxist philosophers. Whether it is truly compatible with a thorough-going determinism is still a debated issue in non-Marxist philosophies in Europe and the United States. But the Soviet insistence on the reality of individual choice (which in their terminology is equivalent to freedom when joined with the possibility of acting on a decision taken) is sufficient to ground a doctrine of duty and of moral responsibility. While many soft-determinists argue that responsibility is compatible with determinism, the Soviets hold that responsibility demands freedom, but that freedom is compatible with determinism. The difference, if there is one, is terminological, since both maintain that responsibility requires the possibility of choosing among real alternatives, and that any such choice is itself caused, and so is in some sense determined by its causes.

An individual's freedom, A. P. Chermenina contends, is maximized by his living in a society which gives him the most opportunities and imposes the least restraint, and by his choosing those actions which are in accord with the general tendency of the development of society, and so most likely to be realized. Ideally a society should impose only those positive restraints on the exercise of individual freedom which are necessary to preserve the maximum overall opportunity for the exercise of freedom by all. This is one of the ideals of communism, where, for instance the freedom of one man to dominate or exploit another economically is to be eliminated, so that all men might be free to develop themselves. Secondly, if a person were to choose a line of action which was contrary to the general line of social development, his actions would be doomed to failure, he would not achieve his end, and so he could not be said to have fully exercised his freedom. Similarly, if he were to choose a line of action which benefited him at the expense of others or of society, though he might achieve his private ends he would do so at the cost of lessening the freedom of others; if the practice became widespread, then conflicting attempts to achieve freedom at the expense of others would often cancel each other out, thus frustrating the achievement of ends and resulting in a lessening of overall freedom. Because of this it is claimed that the fullest freedom is achieved when all men act in accordance with the needs of common social development, acting in concert to achieve common purposes and to allow each to achieve the greatest exercise of his own private purposes compatible with those of others and with the general social end. Since socialism is supposed to do this, socialism, it is claimed, offers the real possibility of achieving the maximum freedom for society as a whole and for the individuals within it.[19]

Soviet analyses emphasize social rather than personal aspects of freedom. However, Soviet philosophers, while claiming that man *will* be most free under communism, rarely turn their attention to the actual amount of political, artistic, and other forms of freedom socialism has already brought with it to date. What it will mean for an individual to be free to develop himself in an all-round manner is similarly discussed only in terms of what society will provide, not in terms of what individual creativity means or of how an individual achieves it.

The emphasis on the social aspects of freedom influences the Soviet position on responsibility, duty, and conscience, since according to the Soviet view all of these factors are based on man's freedom and arise with it.

The concept of responsibility has received relatively little analysis in the Soviet ethical literature.[20] Responsibility is said to arise as a result of the ability of man to foresee the consequences of his actions and to choose among actions which have different consequences.[21] If he could not choose among different possible actions, whatever he did he would do of necessity and, according to the Soviet view, there would be no more reason to blame him for immoral conduct than to blame a wolf for eating a lamb, or a snowslide for destroying a house.[22] The analogies are poorly chosen, for we do blame the wolf or the snowslide, if by "blame" we mean we describe them as the causal agents of the events in question. However, the Soviet claim seems to be that responsibility is or implies a type of accountability or answerability which would be inappropriate if whatever one did he did without any possibility of acting otherwise. If one could not act otherwise, he would be held accountable only as the wolf is; but human accountability is different precisely because man can choose between actions. He can thus be held accountable for actions which he actually performs, as well as for those which he does not perform but could and should have performed. This special type of accountability is part of the concept of responsibility.

The other prerequisite for responsibility, according to the Marxist-Leninist interpretation, is the ability of an individual to foresee the consequences of his actions. One is responsible only for those consequences of his actions which he *could have* foreseen, which in most cases are the most proximate results of his actions.[23] In assessing praise or blame, however, consideration may also be taken of the fact that one did not forsee certain results of his actions, though he could have done so. A person is also held responsible for his motives, as well as for his actions and their results.[24]

If we are correct in interpreting the Soviet position on responsibility as roughly equivalent to that of accountability, we must ask what one is answerable or accountable for, to whom he is accountable, and how such accountability is to be measured.

A person is evidently responsible or accountable for the motives he chooses to act on, for the actions he chooses to perform, and for the foreseeable consequences of those actions. The kind of responsibility (e.g. legal, political, moral) he bears is dependent on his status and on the kind of action he performs. He is morally responsible for those actions and omissions which involve the interests and fate of others.[25] In the moral realm a person is accountable in the first place to himself, providing he assumes responsibility for his actions. He can thus judge his own actions, which is one of the functions of conscience.[26] Whether or not he holds himself responsible, he can be and usually is held morally responsible for his actions either by society as a whole or by concerned individuals or groups within that society.

The degree of responsibility of a person is, according to Soviet theory, a function of a person's freedom;[27] but it is difficult in the absence of further Soviet explanations, which are still lacking, to determine exactly what this means. If responsibility is dependent upon ability to foresee consequences and to choose among them, presumably any conditions which tend to reduce one's ability to foresee or to choose would also reduce one's responsibility. What is clearly called for is a theory of excusing conditions which would establish criteria for ascribing responsibility or for releasing one from responsibility. The Soviet theory implies that a person is answerable or accountable for all his acts, but that he could be exonerated of blame under certain excusing conditions. Yet Soviet ethical theory still lacks any such explicit doctrine. From a practical point of view it seems that in the Soviet Union there is a greater tendency to hold people responsible for more of their actions than in the United States, for instance, where many actions are excused, rightly or wrongly, on the basis of supposed psychological compulsion of one type or another. While Freudianism, to some extent, tends to diminish responsibility in some areas in the West, the Soviet doctrine that human freedom is increasing in Soviet society and that the causes of crime and immorality therein are being reduced results in the Soviet claim that Soviet citizens are more responsible for their immoral actions than they would have been for similar actions before the achievement of socialism.[28]

The Soviet position thus far described is more or less in accord with many theories of responsibility held by non-Marxist philosophers. To stop here, however, the Soviets claim, is to isolate man from his society. For just as freedom has its collective aspects, so does responsibility. Since man is man only together with other men, he is responsible not only for himself and for his own actions but also for other men and for their actions. Secondly, since man acts not only in his capacity as an individual, but also as a member of various groups or "collectives," he bears joint responsibility for the actions or omissions of these also. Though there have been discussions of collective responsibility and guilt in the non-Marxist ethical literature, the topic is of more central concern to the Marxist-Leninists.

According to Soviet theory the collective bears moral responsibility for each of its members,[29] though exactly what this means is not entirely clear. Since a collective is basically a group of people, if responsibility is assigned to the collective, it must be assigned to all its members. Each member, it seems, is responsible both for his own actions and for the actions of the other members of the group, though they cannot all be responsible in the same way. Thus if one member of a factory collective were to steal a piece of equipment for his own personal use, that person would be responsible for stealing. The members of his collective would on the other hand bear the responsibility for not educating its members correctly,[30] or for not seeing that one of their members did not steal. Each person is his brother's keeper in the sense that each is responsible for helping the others live up to their individual moral responsibility. Any individual failure reflects blame on the group.[31] Collective responsibility also develops from certain tasks being assigned directly to collectives or groups. Though individual parts of the operation may be assigned to individual members of the collective, each member of the collective is responsible for helping the others, so that together they might fulfill their joint responsibility. Thus a faster worker has the responsibility of helping his slower fellow-worker, even if it means less remuneration or recognition for himself.[32]

In the broadest context each member of Soviet society is said to be responsible for his society and for its development. Leaders of the society bear the greatest portion of this responsibility, but all members share in it. According to the Soviet view, members of a socialist society are responsible for fostering the development of their society towards communism; members of a capitalist society, according to the norms of communist morality, are responsible for the exploitation and oppression that exist in their society and are morally guilty if they acquiesce in such a society without doing what they can to put an end to these and similar evils.

In some ways the Soviet concept of collective responsibility resembles a college honor system on a mass scale. Not only is each person responsible for his own proper conduct, but also for the proper conduct of his fellows. In an honor system this often involves reporting infringements of the regulations either by oneself or by another. The aspect of reporting on others, which seems inimical to some, is an integral part of the Soviet concept, though in the moral (as opposed to the legal or other realms) there is no one except the collective to report to, and corrective, disciplinary, or educative measures are taken by the members thereof. The collective is responsible for helping its members know and fulfill their responsibilities,[33] which means that each is to help the others in these ways and is to be helped by them.

Responsibility, individual and collective, is closely related to duty, and a discussion of the former without the latter would be incomplete. Duty is both the social limit of an individual's freedom of action, and the basis for assigning moral responsibility. Though freedom is expressive of the fact that one can act in various ways or make various choices, one *should* do certain actions and *should not* do certain others. An individual's freedom is limited by the freedom of others and by the moral necessity to subordinate one's own interests to the greater interests of society, and to choose society's good over one's own where the two conflict.

Duty, according to Marxist-Leninist ethics, is the moral necessity or obligation to subordinate one's individual interests and conduct to the interests and demands of the social units (family, collective, class, nation, or society as such) of which one is a member.[34] Duty is always social in nature, both because it arises from and in society, and because it regulates an individual's relations with others (it regulates an individual's actions to himself only indirectly). In the Soviet view, duty is neither formal nor abstract, but always consists of concrete content, which in a class-society is class content. Duty, like good, is objective.[35] It derives not from God, or from abstract reason, not from intuition or from emotion, but from the specific needs of society and of social organization.[36]

Good and duty are closely related categories in Marxist-Leninist theory. Though logically duty presupposes good, in fact they arise simultaneously in society. Good, as we have seen, arises from the interests and needs of a society and is the expression of a society's aims or ends or goals. Duty is based on the collective desire and effort of a society to achieve these aims or ends or goals. The good or end by itself exerts no obligation that it be achieved, but if a society is to continue and either to achieve its goal or progress towards it, then certain means must be taken. These necessary means are expressed as moral necessities or as the duty of the members of society. Logically speaking, the right or obligation of which duty is an expression is not categorical but hypothetical. Ought or duty is derived not merely from a perceived or imagined good, but from such a good plus the collective will to achieve it. Duty appears to have a categorical aspect because man as man is totally enmeshed in his society, and society's end informs and transcends his own.

Upon entering into certain relations man takes upon himself certain obligations which accrue to him not in his individuality but because of his assumption of a certain relation, e.g. that of father or child, subordinate or director, citizen of a certain state, member of a certain class or of society in general. If the group or collective or society is to achieve its aim, then each member of the group must assume certain obligations and make certain contributions, in return for which he receives the benefits of living in and being a member of the group or society. Society as such therefore imposes certain demands or rules on its members.[37] If one were to ask "Why should I be moral?," "Why should I obey the rules imposed by society?," the Soviet answer would be that it is only by so acting that society can exist.[38] Theoretically one can decide not to be a member of society; but if he is a member of no society, he is not a man at all, since man is by nature a social animal.

Duty comes from society. Just as the ends of societies, their goals, and their evaluations differ, so what is demanded of an individual differs from society to society and from class to class. Duty is objective in the same sense and to the same degree that good is objective. What is necessary for the progressive development of a society is objective, in the sense which we discussed in chapters two and three, and duty is objective in the same sense. Since men may be mistaken in what they claim is their or someone else's duty, we must distinguish between the objectivity of duty and the subjective consciousness of it.[39]

The parallel between duty and good further leads to another distinction which Soviet moral philosophers have yet to develop. Just as they claim a dual aspect of good, one of which is relative to a society or class and another of which is basic to the nature and makeup of mankind, so it seems there should be two kinds of duty. The first would be the obligations or duties imposed upon one by one's class or society. But these duties, it would seem, could be overridden should they conflict with or be in opposition to an obligation based not on the goal of some class but on the end of mankind, and on man's general determination to reach this end.

In either case "I ought to do X" seems to mean that my society or class or mankind imposes upon me (or would impose upon me if it saw its end clearly) the obligation of doing X, because my doing X (and everyone else in similar circumstances also doing X) is a necessary means for the society or class or mankind to achieve its end. Moreover, I should do what society obliges me to do both because the aims of mankind (or of my society or class) are basically my aims as well, since I am a member of the whole, and because my peers will impose various penalties on me if I do not fulfill my obligations.

This is the basic Soviet position with respect to duty. The concrete duty of a member of Soviet society derives from his society's goal of building communism, which Marxist-Leninists claim is the ultimate goal of all mankind. Its specific content will be the subject of the following chapter. But two further points deserve mention here. First, duty, like responsibility, is in the Soviet view not only personal but also collective. It is because of the collective nature of some obligations, as well as because of the interdependence of men, that this is so. All members of Soviet society for instance are collectively, as well as individually, obliged to work for the achievement of communism, and it is the duty of each only because it is the duty of all. No individual could build communism by himself, and so he cannot have the obligation to do so. Secondly, since duty is derived from social necessity, Marxist-Leninist ethics holds that one's personal good is always to be subordinated to the collective good wherever the two may conflict. Such subordination is in fact seen by some to be the very heart of duty.[40] But on this latter view it is not clear whether in a communist society in which personal and social interests coincided, one could still speak meaningfully of moral obligation. A communist society will presumably make certain demands of its members which could be ignored or rejected by some of them. To claim otherwise would seem either to deny that men in such a society have the ability to choose, or (which might come to the same thing) to postulate the complete enlightenment of all the citizens of such a society.

This is as far as the Soviet analysis of duty has progressed. One notable omission is any discussion of the difference between what can be called *prima facie* obligations and overall obligation. Society, for instance, imposes certain demands of a general nature on its members: the obligation to be truthful, to pay one's debts, to help those in need, and so forth. These make up the "simple rules" common to all societies.[41] However, sometimes one is faced with conflicting *prima facie* obligations, and one finds oneself able to fulfill only one of them. What should be done in any given situation can be called overall-duty. Where faced with two or more mutually conflicting *prima facie* duties, how is one to decide the overall-duty in a particular case?

Since the problem is not raised in the Soviet literature, no explicit solution is given. Presumably it would consist of the assertion that one's overall obligation in such a case is the fulfillment of that *prima facie* obligation which would most promote society's development. But this itself would raise two further questions. First, should an act be judged by the general rules of a society or by the basis for these rules, namely the promotion of the fullest development of society? There is no discussion of the implications of either choice, comparable to the discussion in the West concerning act-utilitarianism and rule-utilitarianism. To judge each act not by general rules, but by the overall end both tends to undermine the rules as well as to become practically impossible for the ordinary person. On the other hand, to judge only by the general rules tends to formalize them, perhaps at the expense of the end to be attained.

The second difficulty comes from trying to weigh the *expected* results of actions and their conduciveness to the production of the desired end of society, against their *actual* results, which we may not and sometimes cannot know, but which, according to Soviet theory, determine our objective duty. The problem unavoidably arises in the Soviet Union when attempting to interpret the force and meaning of the moral code of the builders of communism. Almost unexplicably there has been no treatment of this problem and no recognition that there is a problem at all.

Thus far we have discussed primarily the objective aspect of duty. The subjective consciousness of duty brings us next to the concept or category of "conscience," which is considered by some Soviet moral philosophers to be the subjective side of duty itself.[42] Soviet discussions of conscience, like those of good and duty, have appeared only recently in Soviet ethical literature.[43] The Soviet approach to conscience is consistent with that to duty. It has a completely social origin, subjective and objective aspects, and individual and collective exemplifications.

Conscience is a social category used to identify a person's consciousness of moral responsibility for his actions and behavior before society; it is a moral force inducing man to act so as to fulfill his moral obligations; and it is the source of a person's moral evaluation of the motives and conduct of himself and of others. It operates both on the level of understanding and on the level of emotion and feeling.[44] It is neither innate, implanted by God, nor intuitive, but is the result of the historical development of society.[45] As men grow up in society they come to learn what is required of them. When the objective demands of society become internalized, conscience develops. Internalized norms serve as guides for conduct; when one acts in accordance with his conscience he experiences a certain feeling of moral satisfaction and peace, while if one acts contrary to his conscience he experiences pangs of conscience, shame, or remorse.[46]

Since conscience is the subjective consciousness of one's duty, it is properly formed by society, where duty originates. Though a person of necessity has only his conscience as his most proximate guide of what is right and wrong, he has an obligation to correct his conscience and to correctly inform himself about his objective duty, which is independent of his consciousness. Conscience, thus, according to Marxist-Leninist theory, is never supreme, but is always subordinate to duty as objectively and socially determined. Conscience is to be correctly formed by society. It has social roots and never achieves autonomy. To admit the autonomy of the individual conscience would be to install it as a determiner of what is moral, which, for the Marxist-Leninists, would be to fall into gross subjectivism and to deny the objectivity of duty.

The Kantian notion of the moral autonomy of the individual rested on the autonomy of reason. According to this view any rational being could determine his own duty through rational deliberation. The Soviet view calls such a position abstract and formal, and rejects it because it fails to look at the social roots of morality and duty. However, the Soviet position may be interpreted in either of two ways. Either one's conscience is one's ultimate court of appeal, and though he may seek guidance as to his duty from others, he must ultimately make his own moral decisions; or the source of objective morality is society, and if ever one's conscience goes against what society says is right or wrong, one must subordinate his own convictions to those of society in order to be moral. While the Soviet interpretation of conscience in a class society would be ambiguous on this question, there is no doubt that the second interpretation is the orthodox one with respect to socialist society.[47] While the needs of society may not be clearly formulated in class societies, and members of different classes would judge differently concerning actions in that society, in Soviet society, it is claimed, the needs of society have been determined, the objective duty of the members of society has been clearly formulated, and in cases of doubt one can always go to the collective and the Party to determine one's objective duty. These claims to objective knowledge will be examined more closely in the following chapter. The point here is that conscience, at least in socialist society, is to be formed in accordance with the known requirements of society, and is consequently not the last court of moral appeal, but merely the most proximate one an individual has and the one which he is obliged to correct and subordinate to society's determination of his objective duty.[48] This aspect of the Soviet view of conscience is also brought out in the Soviet discussions of collective conscience.

The Soviet contention is that although conscience, like consciousness, can only exist in individuals, individual conscience is not to be torn from its social expression any more than individual consciousness is to be torn from social consciousness, of which morality is one form. Individuals in their moral consciousness and so in their consciences express the interests of a class or of a collective. To this extent a person's conscience is an individual instance of a collective conscience. "Collective conscience" is defined as the aggregate consciousness (feeling) of moral responsibility of a group of people, joined by objective social bonds, for the activity or fate of the given social group.[49] Collective responsibility is expressed in the collective conscience of the group, and personal responsibility and conscience are subordinated to this. What this presumably means is that each individual is to correct and educate his conscience in accordance with the concensus of his group.

Collective responsibility has two aspects, responsibility of each member of the group for the others, and responsibility of all the members together for their joint obligations. An individual's conscience is to serve as a bolster and motivating agent not only for himself but for the members of his collective and theirs for him, and each is to be conscious of their joint obligations. One Soviet author claims that the conscience of separate individuals should gradually be transformed into part of the all-people's communist conscience.[50] This possibly means that the Soviet ideal would be one in which every individual's conscience reflected the objective duties of society and in which each person subordinated his own interests and aims to those of the society as a whole.

The peak of Soviet collective conscience and the final arbiter of conflicts of conscience is the Communist Party which serves as the "conscience of the people."[51] The Party is the final arbiter because it claims to be the vanguard of the people, the most advanced element of mankind, and to be armed with special insight into the needs of society and the direction of its social, progressive evolution. If all this is believed or admitted, then there is a certain consistency in recognizing the Party as the ultimate authority on the objective content of duty for members of Soviet society. We shall postpone an examination of the legitimacy of the Party's moral leadership until Chapter VI.

The Soviet views on freedom, responsibility, duty, and conscience all combine finally in a consideration of moral evaluation in general, though there is surprisingly little discussion of this topic in the Soviet literature.[52] As we have seen, an individual is held accountable for his free actions. He is expected to fulfill his duty, and is held accountable for doing so. In moral evaluation, motives as well as the results of actions are to be considered and evaluated, but it is held that the best way to determine a person's real thoughts and feelings is by his actions.[53]

The little literature there is on moral evaluation concerns individual acts. The question of the moral evaluation of persons is ignored, as well as the moral evaluation of the life of a person as a whole. While the social structures of societies as a whole are assessed and judged according to the scale of development from primitive society to communism, there is no attempt to evaluate present Soviet society to see if it is living up to its own ideals.

Significantly absent from the Soviet ethical literature is also any discussion of punishment, either in theory or in practice. While it is said that an individual's motives, circumstances, and moral makeup should be considered in determining the punishment and education of criminals, there is no discussion of the retributive and utilitarian theories of punishment, and no attempt to analyze Soviet penal practices in terms either of communist morality or the writings of Marx. Forfeiting human life for offenses against social property, a practice condemned by Marx but practiced in the Soviet Union, draws neither defense nor comment from Soviet philosophers.[54] In like manner Soviet ethics lacks any developed doctrine of rights,[55] and the Soviet treatments of justice are few and suffer from acute paucity of content.[56] It is claimed that communism is the highest form of social justice[57] because under communism all men will be equal: there will be one relationship to the means of production, there will be equal conditions of work and distribution, and each person will take an active part in the direction of social affairs.[58] Two Soviet philosophers, V. P. Tugarinov and E. G. Fedorenko recognize in justice not only the aspect of equality but also that of recompense,[59] but here their analysis abortively ends.

Our survey of the Soviet position on determinism and freedom, responsibility, duty, conscience, and moral evaluation shows not that the Soviet views are necessarily untenable, but that they require a good deal of analysis and clarification; that on some issues the Soviet claims are questionable and at best poorly supported; and that there are many questions which Soviet philosophers have not even begun to answer. Yet on the basis of their present positions they have gone on to elaborate the specific content of socialist morality, which they claim is an all-human morality and the highest morality of mankind. The content of this morality will be the subject of the following chapter.

Chapter V

The New Moral Code

In 1961 the Communist Party of the Soviet Union promulgated in its Party Program "the moral code of the builder of communism." It reads as follows:

"The Party holds that *the moral code of the builder of communism* should comprise the following principles:

[1] devotion to the communist cause; love of the socialist motherland and of the other socialist countries;

[2] conscientious labor for the good of society—he who does not work, neither shall he eat;

[3] concern on the part of everyone for the preservation and growth of public wealth;

[4] a high sense of public duty; intolerance of actions harmful to the public interest;

[5] collectivism and comradely mutual assistance: one for all and all for one;

[6] humane relations and mutual respect between individuals—man is to man a friend, comrade, and brother;

[7] honesty and truthfulness, moral purity, modesty, and unpretentiousness in social and private life;

[8] mutual respect in the family, and concern for the upbringing of children;

[9] an uncompromising attitude to injustice, parasitism, dishonesty, careerism, and money-grubbing;

[10] friendship and brotherhood among all peoples of the USSR; intolerance of national and racial hatred;

[11] an uncompromising attitude to the enemies of communism, peace, and the freedom of nations;

[12] fraternal solidarity with the working people of all countries, and with all peoples."[1]

The code has received widespread publicity. After it appeared it was explained and reexplained in Soviet newspapers; teams made up of members of the Young Communist League were sent to visit every family to explain the code's principles; the code has become the basis for some judgments made in the comrades' courts; and it forms a central part of the texts and of the mandatory instruction on ethics in the schools and institutions of higher learning.

The promulgation of a moral code is an anomaly today. Both the act of promulgation and the content of the code deserve careful examination.

We have seen that according to Marxist-Leninist theory morality is part of the superstructure, which changes as the economic base changes. The morality of the members of a socialist society, therefore, should be socialist. We have also seen, however, that a society's morality may change more slowly than its economic base. Since this has in fact happened in the Soviet Union, the moral code of the builder of communism has a dual function. First, it gives formal expression to the morality which supposedly already guides the conduct of the more advanced people in the Soviet Union.[2] Second, it expresses the moral ideals of a communist society which all Soviet citizens are expected to adopt and to live by.[3] In this latter capacity the moral code becomes a means whereby the leaders of Soviet society can help mold, form, or educate the people in the new morality which has not developed at a pace equal to changes in the economic base. This instance of the lag of morality behind economic reality is due, according to Soviet theory, both to the general lag of social consciousness behind social being and to the persistence of the remnants of capitalism kept alive in the Soviet Union by the natural intransigence of some people and by the regressive influences of capitalistic ideology which seep in from nonsocialist countries. The growth of socialist morality was also delayed, it is now admitted, by the mistakes of the Stalinist cult of personality which often transgressed justice, and fostered obsequiousness, slander, and hypocrisy.[4]

The Marxist-Leninist position holds that in a class society the ruling class propagates a morality which is beneficial to it, and which it tries to inculcate in the dominated class. The promulgation by the Communist Party of the Soviet Union of the moral code of the builder of communism can be viewed as a similar instance of a country's rulers attempting to inculcate a morality in its people. The difference between this and what the rulers of a class society do, Soviet philosophers insist, is that communist morality benefits all the people of Soviet society, while the morality preached in a class society benefits only the members of the ruling class and protects only their interests and property. Since there are no classes under socialism there can be only one morality, which protects and fosters the interests of all the people. The supposition is that the interests of all the people coincide, that the good of all the members of the society is served by building communism, and that the leaders merely see more clearly than the ordinary citizen what the progress of society demands, and so can help, enlighten, and teach the masses.

The promulgation of the new moral code for educative purposes is an instance of the superstructure's playing an active role in the development of society. The stage of full communism can be reached only if the people of a socialist society take the necessary steps to attain it. The moral code provides the moral incentive for them to take the necessary steps. The active role of the superstructure is explicitly justified by Marxist-Leninist theory. For while in a class society the superstructure spontaneously follows the development of the base, in a socialist society man utilizes the laws of social development in order to direct society's development consciously and to achieve his conscious end. The promulgation of a moral code is thus defended as one more instance of the Party's consciously directing the development of Soviet society towards the achievement of communism.[5]

The moral code was formulated by ideologues; but the Soviet claim is that these ideologues did not create the code. They merely gave conscious and explicit voice to the actual morality of socialist life and the demands necessary for the progress of society.[6] The code, though promulgated by the Communist Party of the Soviet Union, applies to all the people of the Soviet Union, Party-members as well as non-Party members.[7]

But, according to the Rules of the Communist Party of the Soviet Union, Party members are to set an example in fulfilling their public duty and in observing the principles of communist morality.[8] As Party members, they are expected to be especially conscious of the goal of achieving communism, and they are expected to subordinate their own interests more readily and more fully than non-Party members. Moral infractions make Party members—at least lower Party members—liable to Party discipline and sometimes to expulsion from the Party. The moral code applies at least theoretically to the whole Party membership, including the highest echelons of Party leadership.[9] Party discipline, however, is in practice extremely difficult to apply to the higher echelons, as the case of Stalin so dramatically demonstrated. Only after his death were some of Stalin's actions publicly judged immoral. Even more significant is the fact that since the top Party leadership is leading the Soviet Union to communism, whatever is termed by them necessary to achieve that end is said to be moral. Despite the absence of effective moral sanctions on the higher echelons of the Party the code is in theory the moral guide for all members of Soviet society, and expresses the moral demands of that society and not the whim or fiat of any particular individual. Though promulgated by the Communist Party of the Soviet Union, the moral code claims to express the morality of socialism. It has been explicitly adopted by some of the other socialist countries of Eastern Europe, and, for the Marxist-Leninist, represents the morality which will eventually govern all of mankind.

The moral code of the builder of communism sets forth twelve principles of communist morality. Moral principles are the expression of the most general and important moral norms.[10] The enunciation of the twelve principles of the code effectively answered the question of which norms were in fact principles of communist morality, a question which had, prior to the declaration of the code, been a topic of controversy among Soviet moral philosophers. Precisely how these twelve principles were decided upon has never been made clear, though all twelve have in one form or another, explicitly or implicitly, been contained in earlier treatments of socialist morality. Though the act of promulgating the moral code is without precedent for the USSR, the content of the code is not itself new to Marxist-Leninist ethical literature.

The Party Program claims "to promote communist morality, which is the noblest and most just morality, for it expresses the interests and ideals of the whole of working mankind. . . . Communist morality encompasses the fundamental norms of human morality which the masses of the people evolved in the course of millenniums as they fought against vice and social oppression. . . . As socialist and communist construction progresses, communist morality is enriched with new principles, a new content."[11] The content of which it speaks is new in relation to "the class morality of the exploiters."[12] It is also said to include the simple rules of morality common to all societies, including such prohibitions as those contained in many of the traditional Ten Commandments.[13] But even these, it is claimed, have been given a new meaning, and are now to be applied to all men instead of only to the ruled class.

The group of principles presented by the code have been extolled by Soviet writers for including an all-human morality,[14] for being positive instead of negative,[15] and for providing a whole program of correct conduct, giving man a clear moral orientation in life.[16] However, the code is by no means an explicit guide for all conduct. Like the Ten Commandments and the "law of love" it requires interpretation. It does not explicitly cover every circumstance, nor could it. Rather its most important function seems to be clearly educative, to promote those qualities which are in some way important or distinctive to socialist morality and so need special emphasis, repetition, and inculcation.

The Ten Commandments, given to Moses by God, began by calling for the worship of God. The moral code of the builder of communism, given to the Soviet people by the Communist Party, appropriately begins by calling for "devotion to communism." As we have seen, communism is the highest ideal of Marxist-Leninist morality and is the criterion of morality. What leads to communism is moral, what hinders it is immoral. The first principle of the moral code is thus simply a formal reiteration of what Marxism-Leninism considers to be the highest moral good. Joined to it is the requirement to love the socialist motherland and the other socialist countries. The interpretation of this first principle, as presented in the Soviet literature, makes clear the sweeping nature of this principle and its implications.

Devotion to communism is an ambiguous principle because of the ambiguity of "communism." "Communism" in this context might be taken to refer to the highest moral good, as we have already seen it defined.[17] But "communism" also designates a certain social and political system. The Soviet Union claims to have achieved the first stage of communism, namely socialism, and to be building the second stage, that of full scale communism. If the meaning of "communism" as the highest good were kept distinct from the meaning of the present or future structure of the Soviet state and Soviet society, then the moral ideal could be used to judge the state and the society. This interpretation of the highest principle of Soviet morality is precluded, however, by the official interpretation it is given. For devotion to communism is said to involve both devotion to the highest good and devotion to the existing and future Soviet state and society, and it is further claimed that these two are indissolubly united. There is no ideal separate from the existing and future reality; there is no communism except that which is actually being built. Marxist-Leninists therefore hold that it is impossible to separate the ideal from the reality. Devotion to communism necessarily means devotion to the present and future social and political order of the Soviet Union and other socialist countries, providing that the social structure of these other countries is basically similar to that of the USSR. "Devotion to communism" thus becomes equivalent to "devotion to whatever is called communism by the leaders of the CPSU." The systematic unity and ambiguity of the two meanings of "communism" is found throughout the code.

The second part of the principle makes explicit the love of the socialist motherland and of other socialist countries, and is termed "patriotism" by the Soviet commentaries,[18] where this means a feeling of love for one's country, its people, language, "progressive" culture, the social and state system, and the Leninist party.

For the Soviet citizen, devotion to communism is to include both devotion to the USSR and to the Communist Party of the Soviet Union. By the union of the moral and political meanings of "communism" Marxist-Leninists maintain that the actions of the CPSU are by definition moral. The Communist Party makes up the vanguard of the builders of communism; its leaders are leading the Soviet people, and indirectly mankind, to the achievement of the highest moral good. Consequently, it is argued, the official actions of the leaders of the CPSU are not only political but moral, since it is by their political decisions that they lead mankind to its moral end. Not only does devotion to communism "presuppose devotion to the Marxist Party, confidence in its leadership and authority,"[19] but the actions of the Party take on a "moral-political unity." Thus both the internal and the foreign policy of the Soviet Union are moral if they help lead to the achievement of communism, and support of these policies by Soviet citizens is their moral duty. Similarly Soviet law, it is claimed, carries a moral as well as a legal obligation to obey it.

This welding of morality and politics is not original with communist morality; it was at least implicit in the theory of the divine right of kings, though the authority came ultimately from God. Although most nations and the leaders of most nations attempt to present their policies as moral and either necessary or beneficial to their people, the Soviet claim of moral-political unity precludes—at least in theory—the *moral* evaluation of Soviet policy by its citizens or the moral evaluation of the actual political and social form of "communism" which is being built.

If communism is the highest moral good, work, according to Marxist-Leninist theory, is the means to attain it. Thus the second principle of the moral code is "conscientious labor for the good of society." Work has always had an important place in Marxist theory. The code raises work, which in some views is a necessary evil, to a moral obligation.

According to Marx and Engels man distinguished himself from the ape and became man through his collective labor. Only man produces the means of his subsistence, and it is by what and how he produces that man is defined.[20] Work is the means by which man made the transition from ape to man,[21] and by his work he has developed into what he is today. In like manner, by his labor man will make himself into what he will become. According to Marxist-Leninist theory communist society will be peopled by men who are basically different from the self-seeking individualists of bourgeois societies. The new communist society, if it is to succeed, must be peopled by "new men"; and it is by work, by socially productive work in cooperation with his fellow-men, that the new Soviet man is to be produced.[22]

Work thus has a two-fold function. With respect to the individuals engaged in it, it has an educative function, making them more human, more productive, and teaching them to work and live cooperatively with other men. With respect to society, work makes it richer. A communist society in Marx's formulation is one which operates according to the principle "from each according to his ability, to each according to his need." In the Marxist view production is important because it is the basis of society. A communist society is one of plenty, such that each can have what he needs; and such a society necessitates a continuous high level of production. The Soviet Union, which in 1917 was still a largely agricultural country and which suffered much destruction during the Second World War, has achieved its present industrial prowess by the labor of its people. Similarly it can hope to achieve sufficient productive powers to satisfy the "rational needs"[23] of its people only by their continued work and increased productivity.[24]

Since communism is the highest good, work, which is the necessary means for achieving this in Soviet society, takes on moral value and becomes a moral obligation. Nevertheless, in the Soviet view it is not work as such that has moral value and is a moral obligation, but socially productive labor. For it is this that will both educate the new man and produce the material goods necessary for a communist society. Individual labor for oneself may be expressive of oneself; but it neither educates men in social cooperation and communal life, nor contributes to socially available wealth. It thus has no moral value, and in certain instances may have moral disvalue. As a result, "parasitism," for instance, is morally reprehensible.[25] This consists of a member of society engaging in no socially productive labor though able to do so, and living from the work of his parents, spouse, or others. Included in the category parasite, according to the Soviet interpretation, are not only idlers, loafers, or spongers who actually engage in no work, but also artists, poets, and others, who in some sense work, but who do not do so under the auspices of any socially approved group or who do not produce what is considered by the leaders of the Soviet state to be socially useful.

The obligation to work for the good of society is one shared by both men and women, and is to be fulfilled by each according to his ability. In the Soviet view, women are to be treated as equals to men. They have the same rights and similar responsibilities. Women have been "freed" from the home in the sense that there are nurseries and schools in which children can be cared for while mothers engage in socially productive labor outside the home, though the home must still be maintained, some meals prepared, and so on, usually by the woman. Women are expected and morally obliged to engage in socially useful labor, just as men are, and most occupations and professions are open to them.[26] All labor that is socially useful is to be respected whether it be physical or intellectual, creative or menial. For society needs all of them and each man can make his contribution.

Finally the code makes explicit that work must be not only beneficial for society but it must be "conscientious." This means that it is a moral obligation to love one's work, to exemplify initiative,[27] to avoid exploitation, to care for the materials of labor, to work diligently, to use each minute well, to help one's fellow workers, and to fulfill and overfulfill the state plans.[28] Tardiness, which was once a legal offense, is now considered a clear breach of work discipline, and as such is a moral matter subject to moral sanctions.

While neither honesty at work nor respect for labor is a new moral idea, the raising of socially valuable work to a moral obligation for all, second only to the obligation to strive towards the greatest good, is a distinctive facet of the moral code of the builder of communism. It is however consistent with Soviet ethical theory, according to which a society imposes upon its members as moral obligations those tasks which are necessary for its progressive development. The obligation to work is a direct result of the present state of Soviet society, its need for increased productivity, its still relative shortage of skilled and semiskilled manpower which makes woman-power as well as manpower necessary, and its Party-imposed goals and plans for society's development.

The next three principles—concern for the preservation and growth of public wealth, a high sense of public duty, and collectivism—are closely related to the principle of labor for the good of society and emphasize the social orientation of socialist morality. Just as it is a moral obligation to produce for the good of society, so it is a moral obligation to preserve and foster what has been produced. Concern is primarily for public, rather than private wealth and property. For to steal from an individual, it is claimed, is merely to hurt that individual; but to steal from society is to harm all its members. Capital punishment for economic crimes against social wealth—the forfeiting of life for an offense against social property—is an index of the official importance placed on social wealth, as well as an indication that social good is more important than individual good, even if it means the exchange of life for property.

The principle which calls for a sense of public duty and intolerance of actions harmful to the public interest is a generalization of the previous principle insofar as it extends concern from "wealth" to the more general "interest." Noteworthy again is the stress on *public* duty, by which is meant one's duty to society. For devotion to communism, labor, and social duty take precedence over duties to individuals both because wherever they conflict the individual good or interest must yield to the common or social good or interest, and because the individual always is what he is only because of society, and so subordinate to it in value and importance.

The importance of society is again underlined by the principle of collectivism, which in Soviet eyes is a distinctive attribute of socialist as opposed to "bourgeois" morality. While the demand for comradely mutual assistance may bring to mind the Christian imperative to love one's neighbor and the parable of the good samaritan, the Marxist-Leninist commentators claim comradely assistance as a distinctive socialist trait and oppose the slogan "one for all and all for one" (well-known in the West before its promulgation in the moral code of the builder of communism) to the slogan which for them typifies the egoistic, individualistic human relations in the capitalist world: "man is a wolf to man."[29] For the Marxist-Leninists collectivism is opposed to individualism; and the contrast is at the heart of the difference between the socialist and the capitalist views of man and of society.

Collectivism is based both on the Marxist-Leninist concept of man and on the envisaged structure of communist society. If man, as Marx claimed, is the ensemble of his social relations, then man is truly man only together with his fellow men, when together they share their collective essence. We have already seen the ambiguity in the meaning of this claim.[30] Yet the Soviets insist that by collectivism the alienation of man from man will be overcome and the antagonisms which separate one individual or class from another will disappear. Collectivism is thus seen as a sine qua non of achieving the moral ideal of the unified self-realization of all of humanity. Collectivism is also seen as expressing the essence of the productive relations of a socialist or communist society.[31] If it is not produced spontaneously, then it must be inculcated from above; for just as there is to be no exploitation of man by man, no class distinctions, no division of man into owner and worker, so all men are to work and live and cooperate together—which for the Soviets is to exemplify the spirit of collectivism.

Collectivism, as a component of the moral makeup of Soviet man, consists of a spirit of mutual help for the other members of the groups to which one belongs and ultimately to all the members of society. It implies unity of action, aim, will and discipline.[32] A group or collective consists of members consciously united by the same goal which they all work together to achieve. Ultimately all the members of Soviet society are to be united by the common struggle to build communism, which they all engage in together, and for which they are to be jointly responsible. They are all responsible for achieving the end and each is responsible for and to the others.[33]

However the Soviet dichotomy between Soviet collectivism and bourgeois individualism is too sharply drawn: cooperation, love, and mutual help are all present as desirable moral traits in non-Soviet, supposedly individualistic moralities and societies. According to Soviet doctrine, class conflict and individualism are paramount traits of nonsocialist societies and seem to preclude any sort of cooperation or mutual help in actuality, though the Soviets recognize that verbal injunctions to love one another are present in religious morality.

The conscious organization of society into groups or collectives does, however, differentiate Soviet from most Western societies. And collectivism implies an organization of individuals, a discipline, and the subordination of the individual to the group, which distinguishes it from the view that the individual and his good are in some sense sacrosanct. The principle of collectivism, according to Soviet interpretations, involves the subordination of an individual's interest and good to the collective interest and good wherever they conflict.[34] It is claimed that this does not work to the disadvantage of the individual because in a socialist society collective and individual needs coincide, and society will always take care of the rational needs of its members.

The unity of individual and social needs is easier to postulate than to demonstrate. The numerous works dedicated to discussing this problem[35] thus far all reiterate this and, though admitting that such coincidence does not presently exist, promise that it will exist under full communism. The way to produce such coincidence is to teach the virtue of collectivism. The tendency to subordinate one's own interests and good to that of the collective is not an inborn trait of nature or of character, but a moral trait which must be taught.[36] The new man of Soviet society must exemplify the spirit of collectivism, and this man must be formed.

From the principle of collectivism the sixth principle of the moral code "humane relations and mutual respect between individuals—man is to man a friend, comrade, brother" follows almost as a corollary. Humane relations and mutual respect, however, refer not to all men but to one's fellowmen in socialist society. This is made explicit in the tenth, eleventh, and twelfth principles which on the one hand call for friendship and brotherhood among all peoples of the USSR, intolerance of national and racial hatred, and fraternal solidarity with the working people of all countries and with all peoples, and on the other demands "an uncompromising attitude to the enemies of communism, peace, and the freedom of nations." An integral part of these moral principles, which are claimed to form the "humanistic" core of Soviet morality, is love for one's army[37] and hatred of the enemies of communism.[38] Soviet morality draws no distinction between the wrong and the wrongdoer, and does not preach hatred of the wrong and love of the person who does the wrong. Its humanism is therefore at best limited to members of a socialist society and to those of the working class in other countries whom it feels it represents. According to Marxism-Leninism those outside socialism, by their defense of a nonsocialistic system, defend exploitation and deprive themselves of their human dignity.[39]

Soviet humanism is opposed to "bourgeois" humanism, which, it is claimed, can never be more than partial since, despite its verbal protestations, bourgeois humanism necessarily runs up against class exploitation, class antagonism, and alienation. Soviet humanism claims to be the only full humanism possible because it exists in a society which overcomes all these evils. Communist humanism, however, will become full humanism and extend to all men only when all men live under communism, when there are no more exploiters. It will then be a humanism which postulates the care of man by society, providing the individual subordinates his interest and good to that of society as a whole.

The remaining three principles, the seventh, eighth and ninth, promote moral traits which are common to most societies, as well as a few which are to some extent peculiar to Soviet society. The seventh principle is "honesty and truthfulness, moral purity, modesty, and unpretentiousness in social and private life." To this are added straightforwardness, steadfastness, loyalty to one's word, and devotion to general affairs[40]—all of which are taken at their face value and usual meanings.

"Mutual respect in the family, and concern for the upbringing of children" is the eighth principle of the moral code of the builder of communism. This too looks like a component part of most moralities, though the Soviet commentaries insist that the relations among the members of a socialist family are essentially different from those in a bourgeois family. The difference to some extent supposedly results from the fact that what is sometimes preached in bourgeois morality is in fact practiced in socialist morality.[41]

The history of the official Soviet attitude towards marriage, divorce, and the family has vacillated considerably since 1917. The *Manifesto of the Communist Party* charged that the bourgeois family was founded on capital, on private gain, and on the exploitation of women and children. It predicted its withering.[42] The economic basis of marriage was to be replaced by a relation of love, though this was variously interpreted. For Alexandra Kollontai the family as such would wither away.[43] In December of 1917 civil marriage was instituted in the USSR and the divorce procedure which was established consisted simply of notification that the two parties had divorced one another. The revolution in the attitude towards sex and marriage, however, in Lenin's eyes went too far. He is quoted in Clara Zetkin's *Reminiscences* as saying: "You have of course heard about the famous theory that in communist society satisfying one's sexual desire and craving for love is as simple as drinking a glass of water. Our youth has gone mad, absolutely mad, over this 'glass of water' theory. . . . I do not consider the famous 'glass of water' theory as Marxist at all and besides think it is antisocial."[44] The ease of divorce and the general feeling that marriage and the family would disappear in their legal and economic form persisted into the 1930's when it was officially repudiated and the importance of the family for socialist society became the new Party line. The 1944 Soviet statutes on marriage, divorce, and the family added legal weight to moral pressure in strengthening the family.[45]

Soviet interpretations of the moral code's teaching on the family have not disclosed any strikingly new attitudes towards sex and the family under socialism. Licentiousness and the "lack of regulation in sexual relations" are condemned, as are extramarital unions,[46] prostitution, and marriage as a business transaction.[47] What supposedly is to distinguish the Soviet family from the family in an exploiting society is that in the former the spouses have equal rights, enjoy mutual respect, and marry for love instead of for economic motives, and that the Soviet family is organically united to the life of the whole country.[48] But the Soviet moral code is certainly not unique in condemning prostitution or extramarital sexual relations, or in claiming that the moral basis for marriage is mutual love. While in some ways these views may be an advance over customs which reigned in pre-Revolutionary Russia and in some Asiatic portions of the Soviet Union, they contain no revolutionary moral insights for much of mankind.

Sexual morality is in something of a state of flux in the Soviet Union, as elsewhere in the world. While a certain stability in the Soviet family is considered to be necessary for social development, such stability is not always most readily achieved on a basis of mutual love between spouses. What should be done when love fails? Does love justify extramarital relations, and if not, why not? These and similar questions are scarcely raised and not discussed in any detail in the Soviet ethical literature.[49] Soviet philosophy has produced no philosophy of love and no enlightening discussion of its meaning in socialist society.

The principal aspect of the family stressed by commentaries on the moral code is the parents' obligation to raise their children in the spirit of communist morality.[50] "Concern for their upbringing" means primarily this, though it also includes the traditional moral injunction of parents to provide for the normal needs of their offspring. At the same time, however, the Party program also indicates that Soviet society will play a more active role in bringing up the children of the society by providing more children's establishments "to keep children and adolescents free of charge," more day-care schools, boarding schools, and similar facilities.[51] The Soviet emphasis on family stability seems based primarily on concern for the children; the extent to which the state provides more public facilities for child care, as well as increased public food catering,[52] may in time change the structure of the Soviet family, and so may change family morality.

The last of the moral principles of the code yet to be discussed, the ninth, needs but little comment. It prescribes "an uncompromising attitude to injustice, parasitism, dishonesty, careerism, and money-grubbing." None of these is considered a virtue in any society; so here the Soviet code is not particularly novel. However, the fact that the code includes along with injustice and dishonesty the three traits of parasitism, careerism, and money-grubbing shows the Soviet leaders' concern about these traits which are considered sufficiently pernicious to the new social order and sufficiently widespread remnants of capitalism to deserve singling out. The three vices are considered characteristic of capitalism, individualism, and self-centeredness, and are held to violate both the duty of each man to work and the spirit of collectivism and communism. By specifically mentioning these offenses in the moral code condemnation becomes more readily enforceable by public opinion and by comrades' courts. Some such rationale seems necessary to explain their inclusion in the code; for surely parasitism, careerism and money-grubbing can be considered only among the lesser offenses against justice and honesty.

The moral code of the builder of communism, when considered in detail, is not so pregnant with new content as the Party Program and many Soviet commentators would lead one to believe. Like any code it is necessarily partial. No code can specify every virtue and proscribe every vice; every code must be interpreted and supplemented. The code itself specifies no rule to guide one in the event that two of the principles conflict in some particular instance. Presumably the rule that what leads to communism is right would have to be invoked to see which of the alternate ways of acting would most closely approach fulfillment of the basic moral criterion. As we have seen, however, the ambiguities of this solution have yet to be faced by Soviet philosophers.[53]

The code, as an index of what the leaders of the Soviet

Union feel are the moral demands of the new society which have to be consciously inculcated into the people, underlines certain aspects of the new socialist morality as envisaged by these leaders. What is distinctive in the code besides the fact that the Communist Party is the guide and guardian of socialist morality is its emphasis on work, its externalization of values, and its provincialism.

The moral code of the builder of communism is evidence of the paternalism of the Communist Party of the Soviet Union with respect to morality. The Party claims to know best what Soviet society needs, and in its role as guardian of the Soviet people it sets down the moral norms which the people are to follow. Its paternalism is evident both in the fact that the code has been promulgated and in its first principle which requires devotion to communism and obedience to the Party leadership. The new Soviet man is still to be formed; and in a real sense the Soviet leaders feel they must form him. The moral formation, the education, the upbringing of Soviet man are constantly repeated as tasks of the Party. The Soviet people are seen as developing but not yet fully developed. The parental attitude of the Party is that of a parent towards an adolescent, rather than towards a child. Correction, guidance, and sometimes the use of force are still considered to be necessary. The parental attitude on the part of the Party is an indication that in its eyes Soviet man has not yet reached moral autonomy. He is not yet considered able to judge for himself what is moral and immoral, and still requires instruction in how to act in his new society.[54]

Whether the Party sees more clearly what is necessary for the achievement of communism, and whether the Party's choice of ends towards which the whole society is to move is justified or justifiable are questions which can be raised. Within the Soviet Union the raising of such questions is treated as a parent treats the questioning of a rebellious adolescent: a certain amount of rebellion may be tolerated, but it does not seriously affect the parental judgment about what is right or what should be done. The moral code is to be seen more as a statement of what the Soviet leaders think should be done and of how they believe the Soviet people should act, than as a sociological generalization based on a study of how the majority of the people do act. Some or many Soviet citizens may in fact act in accordance with the code; but the emphasis on the need for educating the Soviet people in the spirit of its principles is clear indication that significant numbers are not yet so acting. The moral "remnants of capitalism and religion" still hang on in the Soviet Union.

We have already seen some of the differences between the Soviet moral code and some other views of morality, including the Soviet emphasis on work as a moral duty, on collectivism, and on the supremacy of the collective over the individual. We can further characterize the Soviet approach as an externalization of moral values.

The externalization of values is a result both of the Soviet emphasis on social morality and of the inadequate and still embryonic Soviet concept of a person or of a personal interiority. In the Soviet view all one's duties come from society and are oriented towards society. In an ethics of love or in the Kantian imperative to treat a person always as an end and never as a means only, the term of a moral action is another person as a person. The term of a moral action according to Marxist-Leninist ethics is not individual persons but society. The principles of socialist morality clearly emphasize society: conscientious labor for the good of society, preservation and growth of public wealth, a sense of public duty—all of these come prior to humane relations and mutual respect between individuals. Public property, not private property, is sacred; the public good, not the individual good, is what is to be achieved. The individual and his good are always to be subordinated to the collective and its good, wherever they do not coincide. The good of an individual and the good of society are expected ultimately to coincide under full communism, but only because it is hoped that in that still distant society individuals will have learned to seek their own good in that of society.

The externalization of values becomes even more apparent when one considers that the highest ultimate good according to Marxism-Leninism is communism, or a certain condition of society. To achieve this aim the present good of individuals can be sacrificed. It is not individual good but social good which is at the basis of communist moral values. In the derivation of lower order values it is always society's good rather than personal good which is considered primary.

The externalization of values is a result of the fact that society as such has no interiority. Society is made up precisely of the public aspects of its members, their relations and institutions. Good and value are therefore necessarily sought in their externalized forms when they are sought in society. Consistent with this the Soviet view of conscience and responsibility are externalized to as great an extent as possible. As we have seen, responsibility is not something individually assumed by a person but assigned by society; conscience is not one's own inner preserve but is to be socially developed, trained, and corrected; and society or one's collective or the Party are to be looked to as the ultimate guides of conscience. The notion of an Antigone right against the state, or of an individual's answering to a higher law of morality than that of the Party is precluded. There is no higher morality than that prescribed by the leaders of the Party. Any attempt to posit a higher morality falls into subjectivism or idealism, both of which are to be avoided. One's good is to be seen not in terms of one's personal development but in terms of one's socialized development, in one's struggle for society, and in one's contribution to the development of society.

Together with the externalization of values Marxism-Leninism espouses an externalization of man which implicitly denies a valuable personal interiority. Man becomes man only in society; man has only a social, not an individual essence; a man is a man only to the extent that he is a social being. All that is good and worthwhile about man depends on society. His individual worth is itself derivative from society and subordinate to it. A person becomes valuable to the extent that he contributes to the development of society and to the extent that he reflects the value present in society. Human consciousness reflects the material world; social consciousness reflects social being.

According to the Soviet view not every human being is a

person. "Person" is an honorific applied by a society more or less widely to certain individuals of that society. In primitive communal societies there was no concept of a person. As individuals began to distinguish themselves from the masses the term arose and was applied to these individuals.[55] The Soviet "natural history of the person" is a purely exterior account of his recognition by society. There is no consideration in the Soviet literature of any qualities as a result of which one might legitimately claim to be a person regardless of recognition; there is no notion of human inalienable rights which can be exercised against society. Soviet philosophy therefore recognizes no personal interiority which is to be respected. Man is man only insofar as he externalizes himself. The result is that anything which separates a man from his fellows is seen as individualistic and so as something not to be valued but to be condemned.

The externalization of values in Soviet morality leads in turn to a narrow provincialism which characterizes the code and the morality of communism as it is preached. The provincialism is two-fold. Since communist morality is externalized, what is seen as moral is not the maximization of individual diversity and self-expression, but the maximization of the socially useful. What is different, what is odd, what is individual is seen not as adding to the richness of social life but as fragmenting it and as splintering society. The result is that conformity and sameness implicitly become values because they supposedly lead to social cohesion instead of to social fragmentation. In Soviet discussions equality is often equated with justice, and the latter is reduced to the former. The guide of correct action is what leads to communism according to the Party leaders. Individualism, subjectivism, and their manifestations are condemned. What is not obviously socially useful in the arts as well as in other spheres of life is scarcely tolerated, if tolerated at all. Diversity is seen as an absence of control and so as a threat to central control. The paternalism of Soviet morality tends to join with its externalization in making it a morality of social conformity, and in this sense provincial. It precludes both a morality of creativity and a personalist morality.

The second sense in which Soviet morality tends to be provincial is in its division of mankind into communist sheep and noncommunist goats. Its humanism is restricted to fellow socialists, and it will become an all-human humanism only when all mankind is socialist. Hatred of a portion of mankind—the capitalist portion—forms part of its morality, reminiscent of the provincial attitude of the ancient Greeks who divided mankind into Greeks on the one hand and barbarians on the other. This division of mankind is accompanied by a Soviet conviction that socialist morality and only socialist morality is the morality of the future, the morality of all mankind, and the morality which will lead to the realization and fulfillment of the hopes and aspirations of all mankind. It is closed to the possibility that other societies might have other moral insights or goals. It is dogmatic and both self-assured and self-content. In a divided world it emphasizes the divisions in the name of morality. Instead of being open to the possibility of an all-human morality based on survival in a world in which there is a real possibility of the self-extinction of mankind, it preaches humaneness only with socialist worldwide victory.

The moral code of the builder of communism is in many ways not unique. To the extent that it is unique in its social emphasis and devotion to communism it may well be questioned as a positive contribution to an all-human morality. It can best be seen as a device of the Party leadership to promote those traits which it deems most important in molding Soviet society in the direction it wishes. Marxism-Leninism claims that all ruling classes use morality to protect their interests and the existing structure of society. Soviet leaders consciously employ morality as a means both of protecting their interests and of achieving their goals, which they claim are or should be the interests and goals of all members of Soviet society. The special uses to which these leaders are attempting to put morality is the subject to which we now turn.

Chapter VI

Moral Inculcation
and Social Control

Since the promulgation of the moral code of the builder of communism many Soviet moral philosophers have turned their attention to its explanation and development. Such writings occupy a significant part of the Soviet literature on morality, and the code is frequently referred to in treatments of Soviet ethics. Yet in the wealth of Soviet books and articles which has appeared since the code's publication there has not been a single instance of any Soviet philosophers' questioning the code, either in principle or in detail, or attempting to challenge or modify it in any way.

The code, as presented by the Party, has been accepted, repeated, and elaborated upon, despite the fact it has a questionable basis in the Marxist view of morality. Adam Schaff, a leading Polish Marxist philosopher, had earlier written: ". . . a Marxist should know, in the first place, that moral codes arise from life as specific reflections in human consciousness of existing social relations, and so cannot be composed or decreed at will. And in the second place, a Marxist should know that the traditional type of code was always formulated in the belief that moral standards were imposed on man somehow from outside, and because of that had a religious character even when they had an outwardly lay appearance. If it is argued that man is the master of his own destiny . . . the idea of laying down moral standards from above in the traditional way becomes impossible."[1]

Prior to the code's publication there was no open discussion in the Soviet philosophical literature concerning the code's content. Since earlier individual presentations of the principles of communist morality had differed considerably, the subsequent unquestioning acceptance and support of the code by Soviet writers on ethics and morality indicates either a sudden and remarkable unanimity of opinion among a usually disputatious group, or the subservience of these philosophers to the decrees of the Party. If dissident views exist they have never been seen in print. The code and its widespread dissemination were quite clearly brought about not by the philosophers under the pressure of theory but by the Party under the pressure of practice. For to the Party leaders morality is a means of effecting social change and control.

The Party Program states: "In the course of transition to communism, the moral principles of society become increasingly important; the sphere of action of the moral factor expands and the importance of the administrative control of human relations diminishes accordingly."[2] In 1963, L. F. Il'ichev, then Secretary of the CPSU Central Committee and the Party's ideological spokesman, went even further: "Unless we eradicate the moral principles of the bourgeois world, unless we rear people in the spirit of Communist morality, unless we spiritually regenerate man, it is impossible to build a Communist society. The very nature of Communist social production and distribution requires a new man, a new attitude to labor and to one's social obligation, new discipline, a new morality."[3] This claim that morality is a sine qua non of building communism becomes intelligible only when we see what morality is to do.

Morality, in its widest and most important function, is ultimately to become the basis for social order and discipline in communist society, making possible the "public self-government" which is to characterize communist society of the future.[4] In the transition period from socialism to communism morality is to be a means of social control initially supplementing and gradually replacing the rule of force. Since the Party is the self-appointed leader of the Soviet people both in the moral and in the legal and political realms, the eventual replacement of external force by moral pressure will make no difference in what is required of the Soviet people. It will not change the demands of Soviet society on the individual; but it will produce the more contented, manageable, and disciplined population required for a communist society.[5]

How this is to be achieved is illustrated by the envisaged

developing relationship between morality and law. According to Soviet theory both law and morality are means of regulating human relations and of educating Soviet man, but they differ in several important respects. First of all obligations, as expressed in positive law, come directly from the state and are backed up by its coercive power: the means of enforcement is external to the individual. The obligations of morality come not from the state but from society as a whole. They are backed up not by the force of the state but by public opinion and individual conscience. Their enforcement is at least partially internal, based on one's union with his fellow men in society and on his own conscience.[6] This is the most important difference between law and morality. But there are others. Law is more closely related to economic changes in the base, and so reflects these changes more quickly. Morality on the other hand changes more slowly and tends to preserve remnants of the old order longer.

Generally speaking the sphere of morality is broader than that of law. Though morality does not necessarily encompass all of law, most Soviet theorists feel it provides the basis for law. Thus while everything which is outlawed by the Soviet criminal code is also forbidden by Soviet morality, there are portions of Soviet administrative law which are considered by some to be morally neutral, though law itself and the provision by law of administrative regulations has a moral foundation.[7] Morality is broader in scope than law since it covers a great many aspects of personal interrelations about which it is impractical to make laws either because of the difficulty of their enforcement or because of the relatively slight harm done to society by their violation. Disrespect within a family, excessive personal pride, or petty lying would all be offenses against socialist morality, though not violations of Soviet law. On the positive side initiative and attentiveness at work are enjoined by Soviet morality and are qualities which the Soviet worker is to try to develop; but initiative and attentiveness are not qualities which can be legislated.

In the development of communism Soviet theoreticians hope that the penal, coercive aspects of the state will become unnecessary and wither away, and that the coercive aspects of law will wither with it. But since a society cannot exist without order, the regulative function of law is to be replaced by the regulative function of morality. To the extent that law and morality enjoin the same obligations all that will change is the means of enforcing these obligations. The coercive power of the state will be replaced by the spontaneous action of the people and by the restraining power of public opinion and conscience. This is the situation which is to become reality in the communist society of the distant future. But in the transition from socialism to communism, law and morality are to supplement each other mutually.[8] Law is first to bolster morality[9] by adding the weight of official coercion to that of public opinion and conscience. The aim here is to educate the Soviet people by every available means in the norms of communist morality and law (where the two coincide) so that they will all eventually and as a matter of course act in accordance with these norms. When this is achieved the coercive use of force will no longer be required, and so will wither away. In like manner morality is to bolster the authority of law, adding to legal sanctions the moral force of public opinion.

Replacing law (at least certain portions of it) by morality has to some extent already been implemented in the Soviet "comrades' courts." In these courts minor offenses are informally tried not by judges and lawyers but by one's peers. The offenses are often violations of the moral code not specifically covered by the criminal code (such as the use of foul language, personal insult, an improper attitude towards one's parents, and so on) and the pressures or penalties which these courts may impose include such social measures as requiring a public apology or the issuing of a social reprimand.[10]

Morality is to grow in importance and is eventually to replace law—or at least large portions of it—as a means of achieving social order under communism. In the meanwhile it mutually reinforces and is reinforced by law in developing in the Soviet people the spontaneous adherence to the norms and demands of society which constitute the basis of both law and morality and make society itself possible. Since the time when law will finally disappear is still far off, morality provides the present justification for extending the sphere of law. Especially in such areas as hooliganism, parisitism, and drunkenness—which are still disconcertingly present in Soviet society despite existing socialistic conditions of production—the teaching and inculcation of moral norms is seen as a means of hastening the disappearance of these "remnants of capitalism" and of lessening the lag of social consciousness behind social being.

The function of Soviet morality in strengthening Soviet law is analogous to its function in enhancing the authority of the Soviet state and of the Communist party. Since the Communist Party claims to be both the leader of the country politically and the guide and guardian of Soviet morality, Party decisions, as we have already mentioned, carry moral as well as political authority. Both Soviet internal and foreign policy, it is claimed, are necessarily moral and deserve the moral support of the people. Morality is thus a means of developing patriotic consciousness and of strengthening the authority of the Party.[11]

In the critical area of the military Soviet morality is both to make service in the armed forces more palatable and to lend moral authority to military commands.[12] The moral indoctrination of members of the armed forces is a topic about which no small amount has been written in the Soviet Union.[13] M. I. Kalinin claims that morality "gives the Soviet State its power of tremendous resistance to aggressors; . . . it makes heroism a mass phenomenon at the front; it is one of the most important elements of victory."[14] All military service and all military action undertaken by the Soviet Union is said to deserve unquestioning moral support because any such action is necessary for the triumph of communism and consequently is moral by definition. An individual war or military engagement is not to be questioned on independent moral grounds, for there are no such grounds in communist morality. Service in the armed forces is given moral prestige.[15] Military indoctrination includes teaching members of the armed forces the supposed truth about capitalism, uncovering bourgeois ideology, pointing out the peace-loving and humanistic characteristics and goals of the Soviet Union, and inculcating patriotism and hatred of the instigators of war.[16] The basis of military duty is love of the Socialist motherland

and hatred of its enemies, and success in the inculcation of "moral fighting qualities" is measured by the level of battle readiness of units and ships, and by the ability of individual military men to fulfill their military duty irreproachably.[17] Military discipline is reinforced by the claim that such discipline has a basis in morality and that obedience to one's commanders is not only a legal and military necessity but also a moral duty.

The realm of work is another area in which morality is expected to exert a positive influence on society, and in which the leaders of Soviet society see a useful tool to help achieve certain ends. The work-orientation of the moral code is geared towards increased productivity. The traits considered necessary for a moral and consequently productive worker are a sense of responsibility, conscientiousness, discipline, and a spirit of co-operation. Moral qualities are those traits which, together with skill, help increase the worker's productivity.[18] Moral work discipline is to replace external discipline and control and to promote honesty, the full use of one's abilities and concern for one's work.[19] It is also to spur workers on to heroism, to induce them to use their creative energy, and to encourage them to take initiative at work.[20] In the early days after the revolution Lenin developed a program of "subbotniki" in which workers freely gave to the State their overtime labor or their labor on their days off.[21] The practice, no longer needed as much today, continues at least to the extent that some workers do not take their merited rest, and donate their labor during these periods in the desire to achieve and overachieve their production norms for the good of society.[22] Finally, the use of morality is a compensation for the dullness and lack of creative work in which a great many Soviet workers are still engaged, since their routine labor is given a moral quality.[23] Supervisors are encouraged to show workers how their work fits into the total scheme for producing communism; it is hoped that when they understand how their work is socially useful and necessary, the moral satisfaction of doing their routine tasks may help to make up for the absence of creative satisfaction in the task itself.

The moral satisfaction of doing one's duty and of contributing towards the moral goal of developing communism is also seen as a means of inducing people to sacrifice their personal good to the greater good of society, to subordinate their own interests to social interests, to foresake their own advantage for social development, and to supply their lives with a meaning which goes beyond themselves.[24] By giving meaning and purpose to life, morality and moral ideals help overcome the feelings of restlessness and dissatisfaction which lead to social disharmony. Moral consciousness is thus to make up for the present deficiencies in the material base of socialist society. Though under full communism it is hoped that each man will be able to have all his rational needs satisfied, the future members of that society must be so educated that they desire only what can be rationally satisfied and derive satisfaction and happiness therefrom.

In Soviet ethical writings and in Party pronouncements morality plays a clearly *functional* role in society, reinforcing law and state action, fostering work discipline and productivity, providing a type of satisfaction to tasks which have few intrinsic satisfying qualities, promoting the kind of family, marital, and other behavior deemed best and desired by the government and Party. But if morality is to fulfill its functional role it cannot be considered an end in itself which is to be freely adopted and adhered to. If morality is to play an important role in Soviet society it must be so completely inculcated in the Soviet people by all means possible that eventually its rules become virtually inviolable.[25] Fulfilling the demands of society must become as personal a need for each individual as food and drink. The body of Soviet literature both on the content of morality and on the means and techniques of inculcating a sense of duty and respect for moral norms is extensive and far surpasses in extent any such literature in the West. In most Western countries morality is taught by the churches, by the family, and to a limited extent by the schools. Children frequently learn what is moral or immoral simply by example and turn to their peers as often as to their elders. In Soviet society where the churches are officially discredited and said to teach a morality which conflicts with communist morality, where the family often tends to preserve remnants of the old morality, and where all citizens must be educated in the new morality, the state and the Communist Party become not only the arbiters of what is moral but the directors and overseers of the moral education of the Soviet people. The Party as the mind, honor, and conscience of the Soviet people[26] assumes the parental duty of educating not only the youth but also the adults of Soviet society in the principles of communist morality. In this respect the promulgation of the moral code of the builder of communism has to some extent facilitated this educational task by formulating the principles; and this is undoubtedly one of the main reasons for its appearance.

The Party and the state use all the means available to them in inculcating the new morality in their people; but they realize that the job is an extremely complicated one and that moral education is not yet on a scientific footing. The need for studies of the effectiveness of specialized educational techniques by social and general psychologists, social scientists, and pedagogues is clearly seen and often reiterated. But though some work in this area is being carried on, the results are still meagre[27] and more general techniques of education and propaganda are employed.

The process of moral inculcation in its ideal Soviet form might be compared to a conditioning process such that whenever a Soviet citizen was faced with the statement "X is your duty" he would automatically undergo a response in the form of a desire to do X. But a moral response is much more complicated and varied than a conditioned response of this type; and even if reducible to such a response the techniques for conditioning a population to such a response are not presently known or available.

In the Soviet view though the notion of duty and a response to it are considered central to morality[28] the process of moral inculcation is complicated and many-sided. The scheme of moral education consists first of teaching moral principles, explaining the source of duty, and emphasizing the necessity of doing one's duty. This takes place on the level of conscious instruction. But such learning must then be transformed into moral convictions, a process which includes the education of moral feelings. Consciousness of principles, together with a conviction of their rightness and a positive moral feeling towards their realization and fulfillment must then be translated into action, and ultimately into social customs. Though in the Soviet view morality arises out of social customs, in the inculcation of communist morality moral education leads to the replacement of old customs by newly formed ones. Moral response, moreover, is not simply an automatic reaction but should involve thinking, understanding, and consideration of the correct response.[29] For though moral principles are always applicable in a moral situation, they are to be applied differently from situation to situation depending upon the actual circumstances. The proper reaction cannot be prescribed beforehand in all situations because not all situations can be foreseen. A creative response to a moral situation is often required.

Since conscience is the basic regulator and controller of an individual's action, the consciences of the members of Soviet society must be correctly educated.[30] They must be taught the moral worth of the end of communism and the obligation of taking the necessary means to attain it.

Moral education is to take place in the schools, the factories, the family, social organizations and collectives, in the mass media of press, television, and cinema, in the arts and literature.[31] It is recognized that moral inculcation of the new norms of morality will not occur spontaneously but can only be the result of an organized effort.[32] Scarcely any means is overlooked in the process. Persuasion is emphasized; but where this fails force is also used.[33] Thus Khrushchev, who was more outspoken but not very different from his successors on this point, said: "We should foster in everyone high moral qualities. . . . But as long as these qualities have not been instilled in all the people it is necessary to reckon with reality. . . . If the moral consciousness of a particular worker is not as high as it should be, then demand by law that he act the way he should."[34] Educational manuals for teachers include special chapters on the moral education of children[35] and special manuals are devoted entirely to this topic. The Komsomol, the professional organizations, and the Party are all charged with the moral education of their members, and members of these groups are expected to teach by their example of living up to the principles of communist morality as well as by their instruction. Individual and collective talks, evening sessions of questions and answers, children's literature and art, comrades' courts, are all seen as means for moral inculcation.[36] Techniques include encouragement, approval, praise, reward, and prizes, as well as punishment, reproof, and public censure.[37]

Most important of all in the Soviet view is the mobilization of public opinion. For public opinion will mold the views and feelings of individuals and will serve as a means both of enforcing compliance with the moral norms and of punishing those who violate it. Makarenko is the guide in the educative influence of the collective, and Makarenko rather than Pavlov is the major influence in theory of moral education.[38] This education is to be carried on "in the collective—through the collective—for the collective."[39] Man, a collective being, is to be collectively formed. By being responsible for and to all the others, each member of society is to become both teacher and pupil. Providing that public opinion can be properly formed by techniques of mass education and propaganda, it can then be relied upon to continue the education of individuals. Public opinion is to correct the individual and to help him analyze and improve his conduct in the light of the collective. The criticism of the collective is to stimulate and reinforce individual self-criticism.[40]

The Soviet government and the Party thus mobilize their official resources for a much more organized and systematic campaign of moral education and inculcation than any country in the West. They demand more of their people in this respect and they are proud of the morality of their social system as well as the morality of their people. In the Soviet ideal of a moral people all citizens would live together in a communist system and would be devoted to communism, working for the good of society, exemplifying the moral traits of the moral code, faithfully following the directives of the Party, and creatively applying them in their daily activities. The interests of a Soviet "saint" would coincide with the interests and demands of society as enunciated by the Party; he would be a creative though obedient, selfless, dedicated communist. This is the ideal New Man of Soviet society. This is the man Soviet leaders are trying to produce. Whether such a man indeed fulfills the highest possible human moral ideals is questionable. But such questioning is not to be part of the moral makeup of the Soviet man, who is to be convinced that his view of morality is the best and the only all-human morality.

Every society attempts to inculcate a sense of morality in its citizens and especially in its youth; in all societies morality serves as a means of achieving social order. The thoroughness of the official Soviet approach to moral inculcation serves as a model from which other countries can perhaps learn; but it also raises some basic questions about the very nature of morality and moral training.

The parental aspect of the Soviet approach to morality is clear from the stated need for educating and training all Soviet citizens.[41] The Soviet people—young and old—are to be raised in the new morality by the leaders of the Communist Party. There is undoubtedly in the Party's attitude some of the benevolence of a parent for his children, the desire to have them do what he thinks is right, and the hope that they will have a better future than he had a past. There is also some aspect of a parent who sometimes uses force to mold the child to his will. But though the leaders of the Communist Party are the self-appointed guardians and leaders of the Soviet people, they are themselves fallible and are not necessarily paragons of moral virtue. A characteristic of the Soviet approach to moral inculcation and education is that it is never finished. Soviet men, according to the apparent Party view, do not grow up to be independent moral agents, responsible for their actions, capable of choosing their moral values and of making their own moral life. Rather throughout their lives they must be guided, corrected, and trained. They never reach the stage of moral maturity where they are free to choose among moral means and ends. They must choose the correct moral ends and means put forth by the Party, or be corrected and educated further. Only the future communist who is still to be formed will reach moral maturity. Paradoxically he will be so completely trained in what he should do that he will have neither the impetus nor motive for acting other than as he should, and so morality will be transformed into something other than it is or has been thus far. Until that distant day arrives, the Party leaders, serving in loco parentis for their people, will continue to lead, guide, and train them in communist morality. Who trains the leaders, and by what right they exert *moral* authority over the people, however, are questions which deserve our close attention.

Moral authority seems traditionally to have been a function either of knowledge or of virtue. Moral advice may properly be given either by one trained in the theory of morals or by one experienced in its practice. Moral philosophers or moral theologians have some claim to knowledge about the subject of their study and gain epistemic authority therein. Saints exemplify virtue in their lives and exert exemplary moral authority over those who wish to emulate them. The authority of both, however, can never be coercive without taking from the individual seeking counsel the responsibility for his own actions and the moral praise or blame due him for them. It is not clear whether the Party claims that its moral authority is based on knowledge or virtue or both. But if based on knowledge, then it may well be in error, since the leaders of the communist party are fallible, as are all men. Its moral leadership may be questioned on factual or epistemic grounds. And if its moral authority is supposedly based on the goodness of its leaders, the case of Stalin is too fresh and blatant a counter-example for its claim to be taken seriously. For if Stalin's actions had moral-political justifications when he committed them and if they could later be condemned (the implication being that they should not have been committed), then what is to guarantee the morality of the actions and imperatives of present-day leaders? The often-repeated assertion that a Stalinist state of affairs cannot take place again because of Soviet collective leadership is perhaps a pledge that present leaders will try not to let such abuses of their own morality reoccur; but when whatever the Party does in the name of building communism is by definition moral, there is no means of evaluating its actions except by seeing whether they actually do lead to what the leaders call "communism."

Despite the lack of moral ground for their authority the leaders of the CPSU exert an authoritarian control over Soviet morality. This is not a matter either of simply presenting norms or principles which individuals may freely adopt, nor a matter of a certain group establishing a certain code or set of standards for its members. But the Soviet claim is that communist morality is the only true all-human morality, and that it must and will be followed by all members of the Soviet Union.

The moral code of the builder of communism, as we have seen, has much in common with many other moral codes and norms; and the teaching of morality and the educating of children in moral practices is socially necessary and laudatory by the standards of most moral theories. The moral education of the Soviet people is consequently praiseworthy by these standards, though one may have many reservations about some aspects of the content of the morality taught them. Some, perhaps many, in the Soviet Union are committed to the ideals and principles of communist morality, believe that communism will eventually be achieved, and accept the Communist Party's formulations of what is moral on the word of the Party expounding them. They must both admit that the Party was wrong as recently as during the Stalinist era, and believe nonetheless that the Party is to be trusted and obeyed no matter what it says or does; and perhaps they do. But for the Party it is not enough that some or even many Soviet citizens actually adhere to communist morality as their moral guide. Since morality is to serve a function in the development of society, all members of the society must commit themselves to it. Those not committed to communism and to the Party must be trained, convinced, or persuaded by one means or another. And it is precisely this aspect of Soviet practice which deserves some scrutiny. Three issues are pertinent here. The first concerns the means of moral education and inculcation. Is there any moral limit to the means of moral education and inculcation? The second concerns the meaning of morality itself. Can a morality which is purely functional be said to be moral, and if so in what sense? The third concerns the restriction of moral inquiry. Is there any moral justification for a morality limiting moral inquiry concerning either specific questions or its own claim to correctness?

There are no Soviet discussions of the morality of the means of moral education and inculcation. The literature on moral education is concerned with the necessity of such education and with discussions of the most effective means for accomplishing the desired end. Such Soviet articles often end with a statement that there is an urgent need for developing more effective means of inculcation. As social psychology becomes increasingly concerned with questions of moral inculcation and conditioning, the methods used in the Soviet Union may be expected to become more refined and successful. In this respect the Soviet Union may well be a pace-setter in effective propaganda and inculcation techniques. But is the use of any and all methods of moral inculcation itself moral?

The answer that I would suggest is that any method is moral which is consistent with producing a truly moral agent. Thus, for the sake of example let us imagine the invention of a drug which renders the recipient completely receptive to whatever he is taught or told to do, and let us imagine that this drug is administered to individuals who are then taught the moral code of the builder of communism and are trained to act in accordance with its principles. The moral legitimacy of the use of the drug for this purpose would depend upon the answer to the question of whether the individuals acting under the influence of the drug could be said to be truly moral agents. If their actions are those of conditioned robots, then we would no more call their actions moral or immoral than those performed by a person under hypnosis or in his sleep. The acts themselves might coincide with what should, according to some moral norm, be done or avoided. But the internal motivation, the acceptance of responsibility for one's actions, and perhaps other facets of the subjective act which might be considered necessary ingredients of a moral act would be lacking. Whether such ingredients are in fact essential to a moral act or moral agents depends on how one chooses to define "moral." But this much seems clear: if the subjective factors mentioned above are prerequisites of a moral act, then any method of education or inculcation which as a result of habit or reflex or any other means produces actions, such as truth-telling, without these accompanying factors cannot be a means of *moral* education or inculcation. If some kind of uncoerced choice and the acceptance of moral responsibility are necessary for a moral action, then any means of moral inculcation which precludes such choice and the acceptance of such responsibility by the agent cannot be moral inculcation but becomes some other kind of inculcation or conditioning. The morality of this type of conditioning, if it precludes moral actions on the part of those so conditioned, would have to be judged in terms of moral value lost over the gain of whatever other kind of value might be produced.

Now if we take this line of argument and apply it to the Soviet inculcation of morality we may say that if this inculcation eventually succeeds to the extent that the observance of the norms of communist morality, however these be determined by the Party, are followed automatically by all the people, then though the society may function efficiently there may well be a question as to the morality of such actions, in any traditional or recognizable sense of the term. Whether the Soviet use of the term "moral," however, is in any sense traditional or recognizable, or whether it is distinctive and special can best be answered by looking at the Soviet view of the functional aspect of morality.

The Marxist-Leninist analysis of moral phenomena yields two different forms of morality: the morality of a people or class which grows out of their customs, expresses their needs, and which they follow necessarily; and the morality of one class which is imposed on the members of another in order to preserve or promote the interests of the former. The Marxist-Leninist claim is that the ruling class has always utilized the morality it preached in order to protect its interests—usually property—and to keep the ruled class meek and subservient. This use of morality is clearly an instrumental use, and can be said to be a means of social control. Marxism-Leninism admits no other meanings of morality. Its analysis of moral experience remains always on the class level because morality, it holds, is necessarily social. It consequently precludes by definition any examination of individual moral experience. Because its analysis is guided not by the phenomena to be examined but by the presuppositions of the materialist conception of history, it becomes something of a prisoner of its own terminology. What can be termed morality is limited to what Marx, Lenin, and the theoreticians following in their footsteps described.

The Soviet use of morality as a means of promoting social order, increasing productivity, developing the spirit of patriotism, and so on, is in the eyes of the Party the traditional use of morality. But there are two essential differences, according to this theory, between the Soviet use of morality and its use by exploiting rulers. In the first place the Soviet leaders do openly, purposefully, and consciously what others did often unknowingly or in a veiled manner; namely they preach a morality which promotes their ends. Secondly, only in the Soviet case does the morality being preached coincide with the needs of the people and with the morality which their conditions dictate.

In each instance, however, the Soviet claim is overstated. The building of communism is clearly—or at least ostensibly—the aim of the leaders of the Soviet Union; but it is not necessarily the aim of all its members. Those who do not have communism as their real, operative aim are the primary object of the Party's campaign of moral education and inculcation. The Party is thus attempting to impose its morality on at least some of the people, though it claims that its morality is for their benefit and will help them achieve what they need, if not what they think they want. Similarly, the morality which is being preached does not actually coincide with the morality that conditions dictate. For if it did, there would be no need to preach it except to the young. Rather it coincides with what the Party deems is at present necessary if communism is to be achieved in the future. And the moral demand of the present is to build communism.

Soviet theoreticians deny that morality is being used for purposes of social control in the Soviet Union since they reserve this term for control of the exploited by exploiters in a class society.[42] Yet it is clear that communist morality is being utilized to achieve certain social ends, and that its utilization is directed by the Party. The Party formulates the needs of society, decides which traits are necessary to fulfill these needs, raises these to the status of moral traits (trading on the various past senses of "moral"), and then attempts to introduce these systematically to the Soviet people. This approach to morality tends to reduce it to a function of the Party. The Party decides the objective criterion and content of morality, it forms the individual and collective conscience, and it serves as the conscience of the Soviet people.

The Soviet view of morality denies the validity of any Christian, Kantian, or natural law theory of morality which presents morality not as a means but as an end, or in which conscience is not something to be constantly formed and re-formed by an outside power but to be raised to maturity and then respected. The Soviet approach to morality follows Marx's conception of what morality had been until his day. But the Soviet approach falls short of even the higher moments of Marx' writings in which he envisages an ideal society in which men are truly free, and in which objects rather than men are controlled and manipulated. The present Soviet approach to morality is instrumental. Morality is to be used to get people to increase productivity. People rather than things are thus controlled and manipulated, though present Soviet practice is justified in terms of the future ideal. Communism is a future moral ideal which is used to justify a present instrumental morality. Paradoxically, when and if communism is achieved, individual and social aims will coincide and communism will cease to be a moral ideal in any present meaningful sense.

To add some clarity to the Soviet analysis of morality we can distinguish three different aspects of morality, which we can name "manipulative morality," "conformity morality," and "autonomous morality." "Manipulative morality" refers to the morality taught by leaders or rulers for certain instrumental purposes which will be achieved if those who are taught the moral norms follow them. This is the type of morality which Marx focused upon and from which he sought to free dominated peoples. "Conformity morality" refers to the morality generally followed or practiced in a society or class. It corresponds to what Marx identified as the morality actually followed by a class or group, and in terms of which Engels could speak of proletarian as opposed to bourgeois morality. The designation "conformity morality" can be used irrespective of the content of the morality or of the way it originally comes to be adopted. Thus both the morality generally followed in the ruling class and that followed in the dominated class can be called types of conformity morality. In each class the members conform to the morality of their peers. It is possible for the conformity morality of the dominated class to coincide with the manipulative morality preached by the ruling class. In this case the manipulation has been or will be successful. When the two do not coincide, the manipulation has been or will be at best only partially successful.

But there is still another type of morality which we can call "autonomous morality" which is not recognized by Marxist-Leninist theory, and for which there is no room in its system. This is personal morality, freely chosen and adhered to not out of mere conformity but out of a personal, conscientious dedication to what the individual believes is right, or to certain values as he believes he apprehends them. The content of this morality may coincide with the content of a given conformity morality, and so with a given manipulative morality as well. But an autonomous morality cannot be reduced to a manipulative morality; adherence to moral values or ends or norms or principles is seen as an end or good in itself, and only secondarily—if at all—as a means. Furthermore, though the content of an autonomous morality may coincide with the content of manipulative morality, the former cannot be reduced to the latter because as autonomous it can be used to judge any action or norm or principle on its own ground to decide whether it is in fact moral. One's standard here may be, with Kant, autonomous reason, or with Christian morality, God's commands; it may be values as individually perceived, or nature and its laws. But in any case the standard in some sense transcends or goes beyond any manipulator.

If we apply these terms to the Soviet Union we can identify the morality formulated in the moral code of the builder of communism and taught in Soviet society as a type of manipulative morality, insofar as it is being used by the leaders of Soviet society as a means to achieve their ends. As in most societies, the morality actually practiced by the Soviet people is in large part a type of conformity morality. Soviet leaders claim coincidence between the morality which is taught and that which is practiced by the majority of the people in the Soviet Union. Whether this is in fact the case is a question which falls outside the scope of this work. But the coincidence cannot be as great as some of the Soviet claims would lead one to suspect. Otherwise the need for moral education and inculcation would not be as important and urgent as so many books, articles, and Party pronouncements state, and as the vast sums spent in propaganda indicate. The aim of the propaganda is to increase the level of coincidence. The emphasis on public opinion and on the regulatory and educative function of the collective indicates that the type of morality the Party desires is a conformity morality which coincides in content with its manipulative morality.

Autonomous morality is not officially recognized in Soviet theory, though it may well exist among the Soviet people and almost certainly does. To recognize it as a desirable morality, however, would be to lay the Party open to external moral scrutiny. It would be to admit its fallibility and to admit the possibility of worthy human values and ends besides those which it champions. Any attempt by an individual to make his own moral decisions or to question the moral goal of communism is condemned as an instance of an individualistic moral aberration. In the Soviet view what I have described as autonomous morality cannot be an authentic morality. For to challenge the official theory, to place oneself and one's convictions at odds with those of the rest of society, to question Soviet conformity morality or Soviet manipulative morality is by definition to act immorally. Morality in the Marxist-Leninist view is essentially social and collective, not personal or individual. It serves a functional role and is not an end in itself.

If Soviet morality is successfully inculcated in the Soviet people to the extent and in the way which the Party desires, autonomous morality—which has been considered by many thinkers the only true morality—will disappear and be completely replaced by conformity morality. But conformity morality is notorious for being intolerant of individual differences, and for being legalistic and morally self-satisfied.

This brings us to our final consideration. Is there any moral justification for a morality limiting moral inquiry concerning either specific questions or its own claim to correctness? Communist morality so limits inquiry by prescribing devotion and subservience to the Communist Party, which in turn prohibits such inquiry. The reasons it gives for such limitation are pragmatic and become moral only if one admits antecedently that whatever leads to communism, as the Party envisages this, is moral. The arguments in support of the limitation of inquiry are twofold and go back to Lenin. The first consists of the claim that Marxism-Leninism is scientific, that it constitutes true knowledge. As a consequence the communist morality which it preaches is the true, all-human morality, and the morality of the future. In the face of this, any attempt to teach any other morality, to present moral alternatives, or to question communist morality is a device of opportunists or opponents of communism, interested only in weakening or subverting it to their own benefit. Secondly, if free inquiry into the validity of communist morality is tolerated the practical result will be weaker adherence on the part of the questioners, confusion and uncertainty on the part of those to be educated, and to this extent the building of communism, for which living dedication to the principles of communist morality is necessary, will be slowed, impeded, and protracted, if not altogether precluded.

In reply to the first argument, however, if the Marxist-Leninist position is true, if its morality is the highest morality mankind has approached, then inquiry will not weaken but strengthen it, showing it repeatedly and in different ways to be true. Furthermore, though it may be the highest morality yet envisaged, this does not mean that the communist ideal cannot be improved, and improved perhaps by the vision of others besides the leaders of the Communist Party. If man's moral ideal is arrived at by rational means or by these together with moral insight, it is possible for others besides the leaders of the Party to make their contributions to it.

Concerning the second pragmatic argument it may well be

conceded that inquiry may make the inculcation of moral norms more difficult. But if such inquiry is precluded, the facility of inculcation will be bought at the expense either of rational conviction or of a moral dedication to truth which includes freedom of inquiry. To exempt the actions of Soviet leaders and Soviet society at each stage of its development from constant moral scrutiny is to court moral complacency and to exalt social cohesiveness above every other possible moral value without sufficient inquiry or adequate grounds.

The Soviet Union has embarked on a plan of moral inculcation as a means of achieving social stability and control and of speeding the building of communism. The result may be the development of a society of moral conformity greater than that ever previously achieved in human history. If the Party succeeds in its planned moral reformation, however, there is reason to believe that the new man of Soviet society will consider himself only as a part of society and not as an end morally valuable in himself, mature, responsible, or morally autonomous; that the end achieved, communism, will be moral by definition of the Party rather than having been worked out by men both individually and collectively according to the best insights of all available; and that the ultimately resulting morality—if morality it can still be called—will be closed and will preclude constant critical evaluation of itself and of the whole society in which it functions. This it seems will be the minimum price of achieving the organized society which the Communist Party is trying to build; but if it is, even the minimum price one must pay to achieve it is too high.

Chapter VII

Ethical Criticism
and Moral Crisis

Despite Soviet claims of forging a morality essentially different from the "bourgeois" morality of America and Western Europe, there are large areas of basic similarity. Soviet ethics, which grew out of Western philosophy of the nineteenth century, is also in many ways similar to ethical theories being developed in contemporary Western Europe and the United States—much more so than either of them is, for instance, to traditional Oriental approaches to ethics. Many of the questions raised are similar, as are some of the answers, despite certain basic differences in attitudes and goals. Soviet philosophers, however, systematically avoid any mention of these similarities, insisting on the scientific nature of Soviet ethics alone and on the uniqueness of communist morality. There is a voluminous Soviet literature dedicated to criticizing and refuting contemporary "bourgeois" ethical theory. In these criticisms the differences between Soviet and "bourgeois" views are of primary concern and they become both magnified and distorted.

Soviet critiques of Western ethical writings are not immanent critiques. They are not concerned with showing contradictions or inconsistencies within a particular view, or of demonstrating errors of reasoning, or of settling arguments such as whether the naturalistic fallacy is indeed a fallacy. Rather Soviet critics invariably take as their point of departure the correctness of the Marxist-Leninist position. Their purpose is refutation and the audience to which they address themselves is not that of the philosophers whose views they criticize, or of the world philosophical community, but of fellow Marxist-Leninist philosophers, students, and those Soviet intellectuals who might be interested in theoretical questions. In many cases it seems that the simple existence of a refutation is more important than the quality of the refutation, or its accuracy. The criticism is

127

not written in the spirit of dialogue, or in the hope of communally reaching truth by criticizing error. The Soviet philosophers' typical view is that Marxist-Leninist ethics is true, and that any other position is necessarily false. Thus K. A. Shvartsman, one of the leading Soviet critics of Western ethical theories, in a book entitled *Ethics Without Morality; a Critique of Contemporary Bourgeois Ethical Theories* states: "In the critique of bourgeois ethical theories, which are incapable of resolving the fundamental problems of morality, the author has proceeded from the scientific resolution of these problems contained in the works of the founders of Marxist-Leninist teaching, in the performance of the outstanding members of the communist movement, in the decisions of the CPSU, and in the works of Soviet and foreign Marxists on questions of ethics."[1] Shvartsman's approach is typical, though she is in fact one of the best informed Soviet philosophers concerning the theories she criticizes. This is to say that she quotes from original Western works, rather than utilizing only secondary sources, as do many other Soviet critics.

Soviet refutations of Western ethical positions are of two major types and take place on two related levels. The first is a wholesale and almost a priori rejection of any Western position, simply because it is Western, and therefore, according to Marxist-Leninist theory, representative of the doomed capitalistic system and dedicated to justifying capitalist exploitation and oppression. The second approach brings specific objections against the ethical theories of a particular school or of an individual author. The two levels are interrelated. The first sets the framework within which the second operates. The second, in turn, is to prove the correctness of the framework by a detailed analysis of particular theories. Let us look at each of these levels.

The first or wholesale type of criticism is based upon the historical materialist doctrine that the economic base of any society determines its social superstructure, and thus the morality, philosophy, and ethics prevalent in that society. Soviet philosophers attempt to discredit all Western ethical theories by claiming the following, which forms a framework into which they then fit their more detailed criticism: the system of world capitalism is in crisis; this basic economic crisis is reflected in the disintegration of capitalist society, with a consequent crisis and decay in morality; the decay in morality is in turn reflected by a crisis and decay in "bourgeois" ethical theory. Any such theory is therefore at best a veiled rationalization of a decadent and dying social order and is necessarily incapable of either accurately accounting for morality or of developing a system of moral values which will be viable for the future.

The economic crisis which capitalism is allegedly suffering is not a subject investigated by those concerned with refuting Western ethical theories. That capitalism is in decline and is in the throes of a deadly crisis is a tenet taken over from other areas of Marxist-Leninist theory[2] which has been part of Marxist theory from its inception. The crisis which Marx described, however, did not lead to a proletarian revolution, and the condition of the workers he described did not get progressively worse, as he thought it would. The crisis of capitalism was therefore redefined by Lenin, according to whom imperialism was to be the last stage of capitalism. This too, however, had to be modified, and the 1961 Party Program of the CPSU rewrote the Marxist-Leninist doctrine of the crisis of world capitalism.[3] How this crisis is reconcilable with the continuous and vigorous growth of the economies of the capitalist countries, with improvements in the standard of living of the general populations of these countries, and with the fact that such economic crises as periodic depressions have by various means been successfully avoided in the most recent past is never clearly discussed. Nor are the facts that it is the socialist countries and not the advanced capitalist countries which in the past decade have been experiencing agricultural crises, that socialist economies are still significantly behind those of the capitalist countries, and that the standard of living is generally higher in capitalist than in socialist countries.

Wealth and prosperity, of course, are not necessarily signs of the morality of a people or society. It is possible for the West to experience a moral crisis without experiencing an economic one. However, in the Soviet view morality and economics necessarily go together. Soviet philosophers thus base their claims of

Western moral crisis on the West's supposed economic crisis, and conversely point to the moral crisis as proof that the West is experiencing an economic crisis. The question of whether the agricultural or economic crises being experienced by socialist countries are indications of moral crises in these countries, however, is never raised. What should be clear is that if, as Soviet theoreticians maintain, a capitalist economic crisis is a necessary condition for a bourgeois moral crisis, then the absence of such an economic crisis would preclude the consequent moral crisis. Since the economy of the major capitalist countries seems to be at least as sound as the economies of the socialist countries, there is no empirical evidence for claiming a capitalist economic crisis (unless one claims a similar socialist economic crisis), and so no a priori ground for claiming a bourgeois moral crisis. The argument, moreover, is valid independent of the validity or falsity of the doctrine of the economic determinism of morality and ethics which we considered above.[4]

Soviet critics would perhaps be on firmer ground if they could argue from the existence of a moral crisis in the West to a claim that the West must therefore be experiencing an economic crisis. But this would be either to say that the superstructure determines the economic base, which is the opposite of what Marxists claim, or it would beg the question, presupposing that the theory that the economic base determines the social superstructure is more sure and certain than the empirical facts which should verify it, though they in fact seem to disprove it. Nonetheless let us pursue the claim that the West is experiencing a moral crisis, for there are many Westerners—philosophers, sociologists, writers, and a great many other people—who claim something similar, whether they speak of it in terms of a sexual revolution, or the lack of discipline of the young generation, or in other terms. Central to any claim about a general moral crisis is both the meaning of the term 'moral crisis' and the evidence which can be or is presented in defense of the claimed crisis.

Most Soviet critics simply rest content with claiming that the West is suffering a moral crisis.[5] The more vociferous, like A. F. Shishkin, denounce bourgeois morality as based on hypocrisy, private property, zoological individualism, exploitation of the workers, and amoralism.[6] A few, however, do try to substantiate their claims, either by quoting Westerners who make the same claims or by referring directly to conditions of life in capitalist societies. As evidence of the inequality, exploitation, and immorality prevalent in the United States, Shvartsman points out that 1 percent of the population controls 60 percent of the nation's wealth; as evidence of the growth of crime, she quotes percentage increases in recent successive years; as evidence of the stress and strain, and the consequent inhumanism of the capitalist system, she quotes statistics which indicate that 47 percent of those ill in the U.S. are mentally ill, suffering neuroses or psychoses; as evidence of the seriousness of gangsters and corruption she points to reports of special Senate investigating commissions.[7] Another philosopher, M. P. Baskin, points also to the number of books which glorify crime, to the increasing number of arrests of those under 18 years of age, and to the "moral degradation evident in the decadence of contemporary art."[8] They could, and undoubtedly will in the future cite the increase in the use of drugs (narcotics and LSD), race riots and demonstrations in both North and South, a continuing series of strikes, and other facts about life in the United States.

The facts and statistics (based almost invariably on U.S. studies and reports) are not to be denied. Capitalist countries are by no means free of immorality or of moral problems. There are many thoughtful people well aware of the fact and both interested and engaged in trying to do something about the situation. Two points must be kept in mind. The first is that the fact that capitalist countries have moral problems does not mean that socialist countries do not have moral problems, though they may well be different moral problems. Soviet critics point to Western statistics to show the immorality of capitalist countries; but that such pointing is purely polemical is reflected in the fact that they never attempt to assess the evidence of immorality in socialist countries. The pertinent studies for such socialist self-criticism, equivalent to the actual capitalist self-criticism found in western statistics and studies, are moreover significantly lacking.

The second point to keep clear is that the presence of

immorality in a country does not necessarily indicate moral crisis. What must first be determined is what constitutes a moral crisis. How is "moral crisis" to be defined?

If we follow R. C. Angell's pioneering analysis in this area, we can define moral integration as the shared common orientation of members of a society toward shared ends and values. Moral integration in a society would be high when its institutions and moral norms are adequate and compatible and when individual behavior is guided by these norms.[9] High moral integration also consists of the ability to pass quickly through periods of readjustment.[10] A moral crisis, then, could be said to occur either when the institutions and moral norms are no longer compatible, or when there is general disloyalty to the society's institutions or widespread deviation from the society's norms.[11] The seriousness of the crisis depends in part on how widespread it is and in part on the ability of the society to overcome it by changing its institutions or adjusting its norms.

But, as Angell points out, and as Soviet critics fail to realize, adherence to certain basic common values does not mean that all members of a society must act alike. Where tolerance is a common value a society can be loosely structured and still be highly integrated.[12] Adherence to its basic institutions, in fact, is the reason why many Americans are demonstrating for racial integration and equality in practice and not merely in theory. The discrepency between the law as written and its actual implementation in the past provides the occasion for many demonstrations, and the demonstrations are indicative in this case not of moral decay but of an attempt to overcome a general moral failing by adhering to and vitalizing the society's institutions.

I am not here arguing either for or against the claim that the United States or the countries of Western Europe are undergoing a moral crisis. What I would like to point out first is that the Soviet use of "moral crisis" is never clearly defined. It seems based on the supposition that sameness of action rather than sameness of orientation with a maximum freedom of self-expression is the only correct norm of a society's moral stability. Soviet leaders are attempting in the USSR to achieve sameness of action (through education and propaganda) based on the realization of the same single, common end of communism. Moral philosophers seem to equate moral stability with moral uniformity. But this position, though implied, is never made explicit and so never defended, though it is certainly not self-evidently the case. Moral integration in a pluralistic society may be both more difficult to achieve and to analyze than in a society in which one stated common end is uniformly to be sought by all its members. Which society is more highly integrated or which is morally superior cannot be decided simply by looking at which is more socially orderly. For order is only one social value, which must be balanced against others, such as liberty of choice, respect for entrenched cultural values, and so on. Secondly, the Soviet analyses of the Western moral crisis are generally superficial even when they use some empirical evidence. They nowhere argue from the evidence to the crisis but selectively choose that evidence which tends to support the prior claim of crisis; for ultimately the claim of the moral crisis of the West is an a priori one stemming from the antecedent claim of capitalism's economic crisis.

The final stone of the basic critical framework consists of the claim that "bourgeois" ethical theory is in a crisis which reflects the decadence and crisis of "bourgeois" morality. The crisis of Western ethics is supposedly evident in the splintering and disarray of Western ethical theories. Their very multiplicity is taken as proof of the lack of adherence to any common moral norms, and of the inability of Western theorists to cope with the disarray or to explain morality and its laws correctly.[13] It is not entirely clear whether the ethical crisis is a result of the moral crisis or of the economic crisis of capitalism or of both. The exact causal chain remains vague. Furthermore, the conclusion Soviet critics draw from the multiplicity of Western ethical theories is not that, in areas of conflict, one at most can be right, but that all must be wrong. This assertion is based not on a detailed examination of all the theories in question but on the prior conviction that Marxist-Leninist ethics alone is correct and scientific.

All Western positions in ethics are considered by Soviet

philosophers to be basically idealistic. Neopositivism (in all its varieties), existentialism, and pragmatism are said to be aspects of subjective idealism, while neo-Thomism and religious ethics are said to be aspects of objective idealism.[14] All of these theories, however, suffer from certain common faults. Since all of them are idealistic they can be neither scientific nor concrete. To a greater or lesser degree they are all abstract and are concerned with abstract ethical concepts or abstract moral norms. If they get to man at all and to morality they deal with an abstract individual, separated from his society and from his social and productive relations.[15] All of these ethical systems are either direct or indirect defenses of bourgeois society, of individualism and amoralism.[16] Neither all of the systems together nor any of the parts taken separately can account for the origin and essence of morality, or present any real objective moral criteria or moral ideals.[17] "Bourgeois" philosophers are the spokesmen for the ruling class and promote the interests of that class. Although they are not necessarily paid lackeys of the capitalists, they may nevertheless serve them by promoting individualism, and consequently the opposition of man to man and the oppression of man by man. They defend the capitalist status quo, deny the existence of a scientific ethics, and so on. Consequently none of them is capable of leading the people in the sphere of spiritual values, and they help keep them in bondage by denying the class character of morality and the moral necessity of the struggle against capitalism.[18] Finally all of them in different ways exhibit a thirst for irrationalism and relativism and so for subjectivism and amorality.[19]

These are the general overall criticisms made of Western ethical theories and it is within this framework that the second level of criticism, that of particular schools or individuals, takes place. We have seen that in each of the stages of the development of the general framework the arguments given in support of the framework are deficient and fail to be convincing. One further anomaly in the Soviet position should also be noted. While it makes sense to talk about the morality of a people, class, or group, it does not often make sense to talk about the ethical theory of a people, class, or group. For ethical theories are usually formulated and held by individual philosophers, not by classes or groups. The average American businessman or the average French shopkeeper may follow, believe in, or adhere to certain moral principles or norms. But it is doubtful whether they have, adhere to, or are concerned with any ethical theory.

We can speak of the ethics of Kant, of John Stuart Mill, of G. E. Moore, or of any number of other philosophers. It is the theories of such men that the history of philosophy necessarily deals with and that other philosophers criticize. Yet Marxist theory in the doctrine of historical materialism claims to explain the doctrines held by classes, groups, or masses, and not by particular individuals; no one has yet discovered all the laws which are needed to account for the specific ideas of any given individual. It is puzzling, then, on the Soviet account to know just whose ethics are being discounted and proved invalid by their general theory. For the capitalist masses seem to have no explicit ethics, and the ideas of individual thinkers are not, strictly speaking, caught by the Marxist net.

We can now proceed to the specific Soviet criticisms of particular schools of "bourgeois" ethical thought. Though individual philosophers or works are sometimes singled out for special comment, they are generally treated—correctly or incorrectly—as representative of a particular position. As a result, Soviet criticism of Western ethical positions is rarely detailed and neither as illuminating nor as penetrating as the criticism of one Western philosopher by another. There is also no attempt to show how any particular theory is the result of the economic conditions of "bourgeois" society. They are all held to be reflections of that society, and if they disagree or contradict one another this merely shows the contradictions which exist in the capitalist world. A good Marxist critique should go beyond such generalities to demonstrate how a particular theory reflects the economic base; but no Soviet critique of any Western position does so in any detail.

The theories most often singled out for criticism are the neopositivist, the existentialist, the pragmatic, the neo-Thomistic and the revisionist. The critiques sometimes show a serious misunderstanding of what the criticized theories are actually saying, and none of these is presented in great detail. What results is often a caricature of the original position, or overemphasis on a particular aspect of it, or a hasty argument about what the theory is in fact supposed to imply or lead to if pushed far enough. Let us look at some of these theories and their Soviet objections.

The Soviet criticism of the neopositivist ethical position (under which they indiscriminately include all forms of logical positivism, logical analysis, and semantic theories[20]) is two-pronged. The first prong concerns the emphasis of these philosophers on questions of metaethics; the second concerns the doctrine of emotivism.

The interest of many Anglo-American philosophers in questions of metaethics, or the meaning of ethical terms and the logic of ethical reasoning, has been largely misunderstood by Soviet philosophers. It is taken by them as an abdication of concern with actual moral problems and as an abstract, uncommitted study of language.[21] Now while concern with metaethical questions may be the sole interest of some philosophers, and though they may not engage in normative ethics or in the analysis of specific moral questions, this does not mean that metaethics is either useless or abstract in some pejorative sense. For it is precisely by metaethical studies that it is possible to get clear what morality is about, what basic moral terms mean, and how moral judgments can be justified and defended. In this respect the recent concern with metaethics has brought more clarity to the ethical enterprise than had been achieved during any other period in the history of ethical thought. That metaethics is the only proper pursuit for a moral philosopher may be claimed by some philosophers; but the truth or falsity of this claim should not be allowed to cast doubt on the utility of analysis itself. For as a result of such logical analysis it is possible to make sounder and better moral judgments with clearer consciousness of what one is doing.

Soviet critics erroneously equate metaethical considerations with logical positivism, as if the term "metaethics" referred to some body of doctrine. In fact, however, "metaethics" refers to a certain set of questions concerning the logic of ethical discourse. It is therefore independent of any particular ethical view. Instead of rejecting metaethics as implying a certain idealistic or abstract view of ethics, Soviet moral philosophers could well improve their theory by paying more attention to metaethical considerations, to conceptual analysis of the terms they use and to clarification of what is involved in making and justifying a moral judgment.

The second prong of Soviet criticism is that neopositivism in its various forms denies the possibility of a scientific ethics, a possibility which Marxist-Leninist philosophers claim to have achieved.[22] Neopositivistic positions in ethics are generally non-cognitivist, and Soviet philosophers lump together the views of Ayer, Carnap, Stevenson, and Hare, claiming that all of them reduce moral norms and values to the expression of emotions and to the wishes or tastes of the individual;[23] these Western philosophers thereby supposedly both deny the existence of any objective criterion of morality (and so take away the necessity of moral education) and promote a radical subjectivism, relativism, and amoralism. By separating moral feeling from reason they promote a form of irrationalism in ethics and a general moral nihilism.[24]

But here too care should be taken, for the Soviet broadside critique fails to do justice to the positions criticized. The claims of the early positivists have to some extent been modified by the positivists themselves, and their claims have come under attack by a number of Western philosophers. None of the positivists in fact either advocates irrationalism or amorality. They are not less moral because they distinguish facts from values or attitudes. They may be wrong in what they contend; but since their position does not negate morality, such negation cannot be the reason they are wrong, as their Soviet critics maintain. They continue to make moral judgments and understand the need for doing so; the importance of moral education continues; they plausibly claim, however, to be clearer about what they are doing precisely because of their analysis.

The existentialists (especially Sartre) are similarly criticized by Soviet philosophers for their irrationalism, which in the case of Sartre stems, as far as morality is concerned, from the individual's absolute freedom of moral choice. Sartre's position is also criticized for its extreme view of the isolated individual, who, independent of social relations, creates himself and freely chooses the conditions of his life.[25] To this criticism of the Sartre of *Being and Nothingness* (and not of *Critique de la raison dialectique*) is added the claim that existentialism in its emphasis on the isolated individual exemplifies the moral degradation of bourgeois society.[26]

Pragmatism, too, is seen by the Soviets as an instance of irrationalism since it denies the existence of objective truth or goodness. Morality for this theory, according to the Soviets, consists of utility and personal success. It thus serves the interests of American business,[27] justifies any action that gets results, and expresses the bourgeois devotion to the satisfaction of material interests.[28] Whatever truth there is in the critique seems to apply more to a caricature or popularized extension of pragmatism than to the theories of Peirce or James or Dewey.

Neo-Thomism and any type of religious or theological ethics is quickly rejected as antiscientific and so irrationalist, abstract in the morality and love it preaches, and dedicated to veiling from the masses their true plight and their need to revolt.[29] The critique here is broadside and a priori.

Finally revisionism is rejected as a falsification of Marxism, as an abstract humanism, and as an eclecticism which denies the Marxist teaching on the necessity of the dictatorship of the proletariat, the necessity of the proletarian revolution, and the necessity of the guidance of the Party in the achievement of communism.[30] In these and any other places where a Marxist ethical theory differs from the official Soviet Marxist-Leninist position the former is held to be ipso facto both wrong and revisionist.

If Soviet criticism of "bourgeois" ethical theories is generally superficial, this does not mean that any Marxist critique must be so. The failure of the Soviet critiques so far is not that they have been necessarily wrong, but that they have been shallow, polemical, often beside the point, and generally poor Marxism. Marxist criticism is difficult; Marxist-Leninist criticism has become too easy. Soviet philosophers have forgotten Lenin's admonition to learn what they could from the bourgeoisie and instead they regard all bourgeois ethics as wrong, to be rejected in toto. Soviet philosophers also ignore Lenin's advice to criticize not in the manner of Feuerbach but in the manner of Hegel, i.e., not by merely rejecting views but by correcting them, "deepening, generalizing, and extending them, showing the *connection* and *transitions* of each and every concept."[31] Only by so doing will Soviet critiques of Western ethical views be taken seriously by any but already confirmed Marxist-Leninists, and only then will their criticism help to forward the development of ethics as a philosophical discipline.

If Soviet critiques of Western ethics and morality have been partisan, however, we should in candor admit that the same is often true of Western critiques of Soviet ethics and morality. The Marxist-Leninist position in ethics, as we have seen, is not without its faults; and the same can be said of the moral code of the builder of communism. This does not mean that they can be rejected in toto, or that, in Lenin's words, they cannot be corrected, deepened, and extended.

If Marxism correctly emphasizes the fact that economic society. Marx and Engels claimed that economic conditions were conditions are important to the life of man, it goes too far in claiming that economic conditions determine the morality of a in the *last* analysis, or ultimately, determining. Rather it seems they are determining in the first instance. Man must indeed live before he can do other things; but granting subsistence he can then do many things. One basic failing of the Marxist-Leninist analyses of morality is their failure to do justice to all the intermediary factors which enter into human action and all the complex relations which condition or circumscribe the higher activities of man. Marxism does, however, emphasize the concrete application of rights and serves as a corrective against a too facile abstract doctrine of rights or freedom. In some instances the so-called bourgeoisie seems to have learned Marx's lesson better than his Soviet followers. In the United States the implementation of the doctrines of civil and human rights and freedoms, which had long been simply abstract, is being promoted. The same self-criticism is largely lacking in the Soviet Union. Capital punishment for economic crimes was reintroduced into the Soviet Union by Khrushchev[32] with not a line of criticism from Soviet philosophers. Until the crimes of Stalin were denounced by Khrushchev they were never mentioned by Soviet philosophers.

One of Marxism's strengths was that it did raise questions about the morality of the whole capitalist structure, that it saw injustice and sought to combat it at its roots. The analytic zeal of social criticism has been lost and Soviet philosophers do not challenge their own society or question any aspect of it. No moral criticism of existing Soviet conditions or practices comes from their pens, though it is doubtful that there is no room for moral criticism. Instead they eulogize and follow the commands of the Communist Party leaders. If Soviet moral philosophers purport to know the proper end of mankind, their failure is that they do not carry on a continuous moral critique of the means being used to achieve this end. Nor is Soviet moral theory used to defend the freedom of the members of Soviet society to choose their own ends now; it is used to force them to subscribe to an end so that they or their children or their children's children might be free in the future.

If Soviet philosophers claim that no bourgeois ethical theory has yet been able to explain the origin and essence of morality adequately,[33] the shortcoming of Marxism is that it has attempted to explain only conformity morality. Marxist-Leninists reduce morality to social conformity, personal life to social life, and spiritual values to social values.

Marxism-Leninism teaches a morality of brotherhood. But the brotherhood and collectivism it preaches is limited in extension and excludes all but the communist and socialist brothers. Marx's notion of man as a collective being who had become splintered from his fellowmen and who should be reunited to them had much to recommend it. It was and is a healthy antidote to self-centered individualism. Collectivism was nothing new to the Russian soil and people, which fostered the notion of *sobornost'*, which saw the Church as a spiritual organism, and which cherished the unanimity and community of man freely united to his fellow men by love in the pursuit of common values. This was a far cry from the forced collectivisation of man by the state or the Party which has characterized the Marxist-Leninist approach to collectivism. If there is a discrepency between what Western ethics preaches and what Western man practices, there is no less a gap between theory and practice in the Soviet Union.

The Soviet emphasis on equality and classlessness is a case in point. Despite the verbal insistence on equality there is a significant difference between the lot of the Russian peasant and that of the successful engineer or Party leader. The desire to free man from exploitation and oppression is a worthy one, but one which it seems cannot be realized merely by abolishing private ownership of the means of production. A worker can be exploited and oppressed as readily by his government or state as he can by another individual. Private property is not the sole cause of moral evil, as the Soviet attempt to dispense with it has shown. The notion of equal opportunity is compatible with a resulting inequality of goods or benefits received. This is true both in socialism and in capitalism. Inequality alone does not necessarily imply immorality.

Finally while Marxism took to heart and championed the cause of the proletariat, it remained always a class doctrine. It saw history as a conflict of classes, and its prescribed panacea was the abolition of classes. It has failed however to reach down beyond the class to the individual. In a classless society the Marxist-Leninist theory has fallen victim to its own claim that the individual will be helped only by helping the whole, that an individual's happiness and welfare are so closely tied to the whole that it is impractical and unnecessary to think of the individual since he will eventually be taken care of when the whole reaches its ultimate end. The greatest failure of Marxist-Leninist morality is its sacrifice of the present individual in the name of the moral superiority of future masses.

The upshot of the argument of this book should by now be clear. Marxist-Leninist ethical theory is not without its confusions, contradictions, mistakes, and lacunae; socialist or communist morality is not without its shortcomings. This does not necessarily mean that any other particular ethical theory is without its own difficulties or errors. Whether there is presently any completely satisfactory ethical theory is a question which I could not answer here except dogmatically, for the defense of such an answer would require another book. I can say that many ethical questions have been discussed in the Western philosophical literature with a good deal more precision and subtlety than these questions have received at the hands of Soviet philosophers. Yet no ethical view can claim a monopoly on truth or validity and no individual, class, or nation has or can corner the market on morality.

In our analysis of Soviet ethics and morality we have seen certain basic Soviet views and have to some extent evaluated these views for clarity, consistency, and the cogency of the arguments used to support them. Let me now briefly compare and contrast some of the Soviet views and approaches with some of those in the West. In a number of cases the differences between Soviet and Western approaches to ethics and morality are differences about fact: whether, for instance, there are laws of social development which have been found and verified, and which indicate the necessary direction of the development of human society in the future. These questions, if they are really about facts, can presumably be resolved by amassing a sufficient number of pertinent facts on which the answers can be rationally based. Other differences, however, are not differences of fact but differences of attitude. On these questions there seem at present to be no facts which can be used to show conclusively that either side is mistaken in its view. If we can generalize, there are at least four such basic issues on which a consensus among most Western moral philosophers differs from the Soviet view. These four basic differences center on: 1) an opposition between a collectivist and a personalistic view of man; 2) a difference concerning the status of man as a moral being; 3) dissimilar attitudes towards property; and 4) divergent views concerning society and its alleged end.

The Soviet view of man, as we have seen, is a collectivist one. Man is the aggregate of his social relations. He is man only together with others. The proper relation of man to man is one of union, harmony, brotherhood, common sharing, mutual help. Soviet philosophers contrast this view with a thorough-going individualistic view of man, with a rugged individualism in which each man is considered a separate entity, independent of his society, and concerned only with himself, his own well-being, and his own success, pleasure, or profit, usually at the expense of others. The Soviet contrast of collectivism and this extreme egoism mixes two layers of reality. The Soviet moral view of man is contrasted with what Soviet philosophers take to be the actual Western mode of life. Western moral theory has long given up the hedonistic and egoistic position of Aristippus. To claim that utilitarianism or Kantianism or Christian ethics teaches such a position is a gross misrepresentation. If we raise the question of whether Western men are in fact more motivated by selfish desires than Soviet men are, this becomes an empirical question about which sufficient empirical studies are not available. There is a difference between the Soviet view of man as a collective being and those Western views of man which place stress on the individual as a person, but the difference is not as one-sided or as clear-cut as it would appear from the Soviet literature.

What I shall call the Western personalistic view of man emphasizes the importance of the individual, his rights, and his freedom of self-expression, and it strives to safeguard these from the encroachment of other individuals or groups such as the state. The Soviet criticism of such an approach is that it is abstract, since it speaks about rights and freedom without considering how these rights and this freedom are actually to be achieved. Soviet theorists maintain that these rights are enjoyed in capitalist societies only by the well-to-do or the educated, not by the masses. The claim has much substance and the implementation of paper-rights and freedom has become a matter of some concern both in the United States Supreme Court decisions and in popular action and demonstrations in the United States. The Soviet view emphasizes the collective aspect of man; but its critics point out that in considering the collective the individual is often lost, his rights trampled upon, and his freedom restricted —all in the name of some indefinitely postponable future time when everyone will enjoy equal rights and be allowed the free, all-round development of his personality. Yet there are some signs, especially in the writings of Soviet jurists, that in the Soviet Union there is increasing concern for the individual in the present, instead of merely in the future.

The collectivist and the personalist approaches to man view him differently. Both would claim that the maximum personal freedom compatible with the maximum general good is their aim, though one emphasizes the ultimate collective good while the other emphasizes the present individual good. Man is both an individual and a social being, and it is not clear what facts if any are relevant to change one's attitude from emphasizing one or the other aspect of man. Inherent in these different attitudes are differences in their conceptions of man as a moral being and in their views on property.

The Soviet approach to morality, as we have seen, is basically social, and man is to achieve moral maturity only in the future communistic society. Soviet man in the present is considered to be in constant need of moral education and reeducation. The good of society is more important than individual good; it goes beyond individual competence to gauge, and so must be gauged by the leaders of society. They determine society's needs; and it is the needs of society that serve as the proximate objective criterion of good and duty. Soviet man must therefore be told his duty. His moral education is never completed and is in the hands of the leaders of the society—the leaders of the Communist Party of the Soviet Union.

In most Western views which emphasize the individual person, man is held to require moral education only until he achieves maturity. It is not maturity of the human race in some future period that is considered, but the maturity of each individual of the society. When the individual reaches maturity he is considered (save in exceptional cases) morally competent. With his individual physical, emotional, and mental maturity, he is considered to achieve moral maturity as well. As a mature moral agent he is to be allowed a maximum of freedom of action compatible with the freedom of others, with the understanding that he is responsible for the exercise of his freedom. Being morally mature he is no longer expected to require constant moral education, but is expected to grow morally just as he grows in other areas of knowledge and action. He does not have to be told constantly what to do but should be able to decide his actions for himself. He may be required to work for the common good, but he is allowed to work for his own good as well.

As in the previous case it is again not clear precisely what sort of facts would enable one to decide whether the men of a society are morally mature or require constant moral education. If no set of facts seems sufficient to prove that a certain group in a society is by right the sole competent judge and tutor of the other adults in that society, it is difficult to imagine any set of facts which would change the mind of one who believes there is such a group. For the difference hinges on different evaluations of facts and not on the facts themselves.

The Marxist-Leninist attitude towards private property, as is well known, differs sharply from that prevalent in most Western views. According to these views the ownership of private property is not an evil, but a good, a right which an individual can legitimately exercise. Individual initiative is seen as deserving the reasonable rewards it may reap. Private ownership of the means of production and competition are seen (with some exceptions) as the means of achieving the greatest productive efficiency and consumer satisfaction. The role of government is to prevent abuses; but it is best able to do so only if it itself is not the only producer or the sole owner of the means of production.

To Marxist-Leninist eyes, however, private property, or more exactly the private ownership of the means of production, is one of the root causes of immorality. It enables the owners of the means of production to exploit and oppress the employees. It leads to vast inequalities—excessive personal wealth for a few and poverty for many. A society based on private property leads also to excessive concern with things, objects, property, and money, at the expense of concern with people; in such a society greed dominates. As a result men do not share with each other; they seek personal gain and profit at the expense of others. Property thus separates man from man. With the abolition of private property and the private ownership of the means of production, these evils are wiped away. The critic of communism is quick to reply that even if this were true, Soviet history has shown that other evils are quick to take their place, and that the evils of a private-property, capitalist system are easier to control and minimize than the evils of an all-powerful government which attempts to manage all of society, control all of production, and which has no limitations placed upon it. Domination of all individuals by the state is worse than domination of some individuals by other individuals, providing the state can at least enter in and control the most flagrant abuses.

Both private property and state power can be abused, and both can lead to immorality. Probably both sides would agree here. However, while the Marxist-Leninists consider private property so morally dangerous as necessarily to corrupt any social system built upon it, this is denied by most Westerners, though many of them would admit that there are moral abuses and dangers that go along with it. They see these dangers as controllable and as compatible with the other goods and values they choose and aspire towards. They see antitrust and similar laws, graduated income taxes, inheritance and other taxes, and powerful unions as means of controlling the private owners of production, and more subtle moral influences as means of controlling individual greed. In any event many Westerners evidently think that the evils which go with a modified free enterprise system are preferable to those which accompany other systems. Many Soviets also undoubtedly prefer their system and see it as possible of being abused but as less morally dangerous and more able to fulfill their needs than any other system.

With respect to property and power the moral choice is again neither all white nor all black. Both can be abused, and the Soviets and the West seem to have made different choices as to which is a source of greater immorality and which offers the greatest hope of achieving their desires. Each morally condemns aspects of the other system and there seems to be no clear set of facts which one could compile at this time to change the views or choice of either side.

The fourth basic disagreement concerns the moral end of man as envisaged by the Marxist-Leninists and by most Western views. Here the issue is related to the notions of man which we discussed above. According to Marxism-Leninism, there is one ultimate moral end of man, namely communism. This is said to be the only proper moral end of man, the one which all men desire whether they realize it or not, and the one which will finally be achieved by all mankind. In terms of this holistic, moral future end, man must be willing to be led by those best qualified to lead mankind, which according to Marxism-Leninism, is the Communist Party and especially its leaders.

Opposed to this is a pluralistic view of man and of his ends. In the West there is no consensus about what man's end is, and no unanimity about any particular, single end. While most men would probably desire human life on the whole to be better in all possible ways, and would join together for the promotion of the common good, they do not believe that any group of men is especially endowed with knowledge about what is good for all men or with knowledge of how to produce it. If each man is morally mature and can within limits choose his own end, then there can be said to be no one final end which all men must follow or which is the true end for all men. If, for "communism" we substitute the idea of a society in which there is no oppression or exploitation, in which each man has what he needs and is able to develop his capacities to the fullest extent, in which the good of each is compatible with the good of all and men live in peace and brotherhood, most men would probably not deny that this is a worthwhile goal. Many Westerners reject not this end, though they may deny the possibility of attaining it, but the means by which the Communist Party is attempting to achieve this end.

The communist ideal society is not unique to communism or communists and is at least nominally consistent with the Greco-Roman and Judeo-Christian traditions. There is no inconsistency in principle between this end and a rationally planned and regulated society, given sufficient knowledge, though the argument from complexity suggests that no one presently has sufficient knowledge to make the end a reality within the foreseeable future. To critics there is a discrepancy between means and end in the present Soviet endeavor.

The attempt to inculcate communist values in the Soviet people, to enforce adherence to the new moral code of the builder of communism, to limit the development of the arts within the boundaries of socialist realism are all explicable in terms of a Soviet attempt to develop social stability, to replace force by public opinion and the internal voice of conscience. Social stability if thus achieved is reached by means of imposed social control. The result is stability at the expense of diversity, and all conformity—even if within fairly wide limits—is preserved at the expense of possible future innovation. Creativity can neither be commanded nor rationally predicted; to predict it would be to know in advance what would be produced, and so would preclude the possibility of its being true creativity in the future. In the attempt at total planning morality is included in the Soviet plan not as something to be fostered for its own sake but as something to be used to help achieve social control, to strengthen observance of socialist legality, to secure popular support for political decisions, to motivate initiative at work, and willingly to put the general good before one's own wherever the two conflict. However, if morality is a tool of social control manipulated by leaders to achieve certain ends, then the traditional concept of morality and of moral value has been undermined and replaced by some other values. The attempt to achieve the moral end of communism by this means is extremely paradoxical, if not contradictory. If the price of social control and the achievement of the end of communism is the loss of creativity, morality, and the personal sphere, then the price is too high. This claim is obviously a value judgment, however; again no facts are sufficient to force the consent of someone who holds the opposite view.

The Soviet approach to the building of the new society implies an all-knowing or almost all-knowing group leading society and helping it develop and advance by utilizing its knowledge in order to achieve a common end. It neglects individual rationality, enjoyed by individuals, which, as far as we know, progresses by opposition, criticism, and discussion, and which is fostered by diversity of values, ends, and approaches. If rationality as individually experienced does grow by criticism and discussion, and if man's collective knowledge proceeds in the same way, then there appears to be a certain incompatibility between it and the ideal of social control. For the rationality of the whole precludes the enjoyment of rational growth and enlightenment by the parts.

Soviet philosophers use an organic model for envisaging society, taken collectively. If the model is erroneous, each man is (or at least many men are) capable of rational decision and free choice, and there is little justification for any group's speaking, thinking, or planning for the whole unless the group can show that its information is better than that of the individual and that it will in fact achieve what the individual wants better than he himself can. Or, if the model is correct and useful, then in fact some men should properly by designated certain drone tasks, and freedom and rationality, at least until the ultimate end is reached, should be restricted to special members or portions of the whole organism. Such an organization is imaginable, and may be produced. But the question is whether the values achieved in such a society compensate for those which are necessarily lost, both on the road to the achievement of the final end and within the actually realized society itself. The answer of those who reject Marxism-Leninism is negative, that of the Marxist-Leninists is positive.

If the Soviet and Western approaches to morality are as I have briefly outlined them, if there are some similarities and some serious differences in attitude, there is one more question which has to be raised, though I cannot pretend to do more than raise it here. In a world rapidly shrinking as a result of the rapidity of communication and transportation and of the span of missiles, are the two moral attitudes we have contrasted either sufficiently similar or sufficiently compatible to help form a basis for a truly human morality?

If we return to the concept of moral crisis, a good case can be made for the claim that it is neither the West nor the Soviet Union nor any other nation or group of nations alone but the world as a whole that is in a state of moral crisis. For there are no institutions adequate to common world needs, the most obvious of which is human survival in an age where human annihilation is an ever-present reality. North America and Europe, including the Soviet Union, form the "have" part of the world, while most of Asia, Africa, and large portions of South America form the "have not" part. The global inequities are as extreme as those which Marx decried in the capitalist countries of the 19th century. Yet both Soviet and most Western moralists seem relatively complacent about the global inequity and moral crisis which transcends borders. Soviet and Western moralities must be stretched if a solution is to be found. All claim to be all-human moralities; but none in fact is.

A truly all-human morality is necessary not only for the future but also for the present, and might possibly be based on general human survival and other common needs. If social stability is one of the aims and purposes of social morality, its need on a worldwide scale is now more imperative than ever. International law based on even a minimal common moral all-human consensus is preferable to either international lawlessness or our present precarious balance of power.

The aims of humanity are broader, larger, wider, and more varied than those set by any country or Party, communist or other. Despite some common needs and aims, therefore, a global morality must allow for real divergencies. Coexistence requires a tolerance for the views, aims, goals, and values of others, which is incompatible with a doctrine that claims to speak for all humanity and attempts to impose its views, aims, goals, and values on all mankind. To the extent that Soviet morality attempts to do this, and is backed by the power of the Soviet state, it is incompatible with a global morality tolerant of different aims and values. As it presently stands, communist morality is a morality for part of a politically restricted world.

If Soviet ethics is monolithic and if Soviet official morality is provincial and dogmatic, this does not mean that Marxist ethics and communist morality must necessarily go the present Soviet way. Some Polish, Hungarian and Yugoslav Marxists have shown that by basing their theory on the early, humanistic works of Marx, and by rethinking Marx in the light of present conditions it is possible to produce a Marxist ethics and a socialist morality which are neither as provincial nor as dogmatic as the

Soviet model.[34] However, at present there is no indication of a change in attitude on the part of Soviet philosophers or leaders. Soviet ethics gives every indication that it will continue along the uninspired and relatively unimaginative Marx-Engels-Leninist road it has followed for the past decade; and the moral principles listed in the code of the builder of communism will continue to be the heart of the morality paternally inculcated into the Soviet people by their leaders. This might be disappointing to those hopeful for a fruitful philosophical dialogue with Soviet philosophers or for an early solution to a worldwide moral dilemma. Nevertheless, it seems to be a fact which these and others must face and live with for the indefinite future.

Notes

Notes to Chapter 1

1. See, for example, A. F. Shishkin, *Osnovy marksistskoi etiki* [*Fundamentals of Marxist Ethics*] (Moskva: Izd. IMO, 1961), p. 43, and the anthology, V. I. Lenin, *O kommunisticheskoi nravstvennosti* [*On Communist Morals*] (Moskva: Gos. Izd. Politicheskoi literatury, 1961).

2. For a classification and discussion of some of these attempts see George L. Kline, "Leszek Kolakowski and the Revision of Marxism," *European Philosophy Today*, George L. Kline (ed.) (Chicago, Quadrangle Books, 1965). For two of the few Soviet discussions of the history of ethics in the Soviet Union see G. A. Gontarev, A. L. Khaikin, "Razvitie marksistskoi ethicheskoi mysli v SSSR" [The Development of Marxist Ethical Thought in the USSR], *Filosofskie nauki* [*Philosophical Sciences*], 1967, 5, 79-87; A. G. Kharchev, B. D. Iakovlev, "Razvitie marksistsko-leninskoi etiki v gody stroitel'stva sotsializma v SSSR" [The Development of Marxist-Leninist Ethics in the Years of Building Socialism in the USSR], *Voprosy filosofii* [*Problems of Philosophy*], 1968, 4, 3-12.

3. Richard T. De George, *Patterns of Soviet Thought* (Ann Arbor: University of Michigan Press, 1966), pp. 188-89; Gustav A. Wetter, *Dialectical Materialism* (New York: Praeger, 1958), pp. 183-89; J. M. Bochenski, *Soviet Russian Dialectical Materialism* (Dordrecht: D. Reidel Publishing Co., 1963), pp. 38-41.

4. See De George, op. cit., pp. 194-98; Wetter, op. cit., pp. 196-201.

5. Engels to Bloch, Sept. 21-22, 1890. Karl Marx and Frederick Engels, *Selected Correspondence* (Moscow: Foreign Languages Publishing House), pp. 498-500.

6. These manuscripts were first published in full in 1932. A portion of them had been published in Russian in 1927.

7. The first Marxist-Leninist work in value theory was V. P. Tugarinov, *O tsennostiakh zhizni i kul'tury* [On the Values of Life and

Culture] (Leningrad: Izd. Leningradskogo Universiteta, 1960). Since then a number of articles have appeared on this topic. See below, p. 156, note 27.

8. For a discussion of the relation of ideology and philosophy see De George, op. cit., pp. 226-33; also George Fischer (ed.), *Science and Ideology in Soviet Society* (New York: Atherton Press, 1967), pp. 48-52.

Notes to Chapter II

1. A. F. Shishkin, *Osnovy marksistskoi etiki,* p. 15; *Filosofskii slovar'* [Philosophical Dictionary], pod. red. M. M. Rozentalia i P. F. Iudina (Moskva: Izd. Politicheskoi Literatury, 1963), p. 530.

2. *O kommunisticheskoi etike* [On Communist Ethics] (Leningrad, 1962), pp. 5-35; S. Utkin, *Ocherki po marksistsko-leninskoi etike* [Essays on Marxist-Leninist Ethics] (Moskva: Izd. sotsial'no-ekonomicheskoi literatury, 1962), pp. 18, 23; E. G. Fedorenko, *Osnovy marksistsko-leninskoi etiki* [Fundamentals of Marxist-Leninist Ethics] (Kiev: Izd. Kievskogo Un-ta, 1965), p. 19; V. G. Ivanov, N. V. Rybakova, *Ocherki marksistsko-leninskoi etiki* [Essays on Marxist-Leninist Ethics] (Leningrad: Izd. Leningradskogo Un-ta, 1963), p. 18.

3. A. F. Shishkin, "O predmete etiki kak nauki" [On the Subject of Ethics as a Science], *Voprosy filosofii,* 1964, 1, p. 27; *Filosofskii slovar',* p. 530; Ivanov and Rybakova, op. cit., p. 18.

4. Shishkin, art. cit., p. 27; *Kratkii slovar' po etiki* [Short Dictionary of Ethics], pod red. O. G. Drobnitskogo i I. S. Kona (Moskva: Izd. Politicheskoi Literatury, 1965), pp. 217-18, identifies metaethics with neopositivism, as does the article in *Filosofskii slovar',* p. 267.

5. *Osnovy marksistskoi filosofii* [Fundamentals of Marxist Philosophy], izd. 2-e (Moskva: Izd. Politicheskoi Literatury, 1964), p. 556; Ivanov and Rybakova, op. cit., pp. 23-45; Utkin, op. cit., pp. 78-81.

6. *Filosofskii slovar',* p. 318.

7. *Karl Marx, Friedrich Engels, Werke* (Berlin: Dietz Verlag), 3, pp. 26-27 (English translation, Karl Marx and Friedrich Engels, *The German Ideology* (Moscow: Progress Publishers, 1964), pp. 37-38.

8. *Ibid.,* p. 30 (Eng. trans., p. 42).

9. *Ibid.,* p. 21 (Eng. trans., p. 31).

10. *Ibid.,* (Eng. trans., p. 32).

11. Shishkin, op. cit., pp. 34-43.

12. *Ibid.,* p. 7. S. V. Kurylev, "Moral' i ee mesto v sisteme sotsial'-nykh norm" [Morality and Its Place in the System of Social Norms], *Voprosy filosofii,* 1966, 9, pp. 15-23, attempts, unsuccessfully, to differentiate moral from other social norms. For a discussion of various definitions of "morality" suggested in the Soviet literature, see Ivanov and Rybakova, pp. 23 ff. The authors of this book distinguish between 'moral' ' and 'nravstvennost' ' (pp. 23-24). Shishkin, art. cit., pp. 25-26 claims, however, that this distinction was not made by Marx, Engels, and Lenin, and so should not be made by Soviet philosophers.

13. Shishkin, op. cit., pp. 56-60; Ivanov and Rybakova, pp. 49-52; Fedorenko, op. cit., pp. 21-26. The precise way and time in which morality developed and whether its first appearance is contemporaneous with the appearance of social labor or later is disputed in the Soviet literature. For a résumé and a defense of the latter position see A. A. Guseinov, "Problema proiskhozhdeniia nravstvennosti" [The Problem of the Origin of Morality], *Filosofskie nauki,* 1964, 3, pp. 57-66.

14. For the historical development of morality in its various periods see Shishkin, op. cit., Chapter II; Fedorenko, op. cit., Chapter II; Utkin, op. cit., Chapter II; Ivanov and Rybakova, pp. 46-118.

15. Shishkin, op. cit., pp. 106-9; V. Afanaseyev, *Marxist Philosophy* (Moscow: Foreign Languages Publishing House), pp. 356-75; *Osnovy marksistskoi filosofii,* pp. 577-83.

16. *Osnovy marksistskoi filosofii,* p. 564; Shishkin, *op. cit.,* pp. 428-38; Tugarinov, *O tsennostiakh zhizni i kul 'tury,* p. 127; Fedorenko, op. cit., pp. 58-65; I. Kyz'minkov, "Kommunisticheskaia moral' i obshchechelovecheskie normy nravstvennosti" [Communist Morality and Universal Moral Norms], *Kommunist,* 1964, 1, pp. 86-95.

17. Idem.

18. Ivanov and Rybakova, p. 19.

19. See Kurylev, art. cit.; Ivanov and Rybakova, pp. 23-45, give a summary of various Soviet views on how to distinguish morality as a separate kind of social consciousness. None of these is wholly satisfactory.

20. Marx, Engels, *Werke,* 3, p. 534 (English translation, *The German Ideology,* p. 652).

21. Marx, Engels, *Werke,* 3, p. 21 (Eng. trans., p. 32).

22. See P. N. Fedoseev, "Humanism and the Modern World," *Philosophy, Science and Man: The Soviet Delegation Reports for the XIII World Congress of Philosophy* (Moscow: The Academy of Sciences of the USSR, 1963), pp. 22-23; Shishkin, op. cit., p. 324. For a fuller discussion of this point see Richard T. De George, "The Soviet Concept of Man," *Studies in Soviet Thought,* IV (1964), pp. 261-76.

23. See the references mentioned in note 14 above.

24. The relation of the division of labor, private property, and alienation is somewhat ambiguous in the writings of Marx. In *Economic and Philosophic Manuscripts of 1844* Marx claims the division of labor makes man one-sided (*Marx Engels Gesamtausgabe* (Berlin: Marx-Engels-Verlag), 1:3, p. 25; English translation: Moscow: Foreign Languages Publishing House, 1961, p. 25), and says that private property is at least initially the product of alienated labor (*ibid.,* pp. 91-92; Eng. trans., p. 80). In *The German Ideology* Marx and Engels speak of the division of labor developing naturally. It takes on negative aspects only later, and brings with it unequal distribution and private property. They then equate the division of labor and private property (*Werke,* 3, pp. 31-33; Eng. trans., pp. 42-44). Whether all three are necessarily evil, whether any of the three might exist in some form without the other two, and whether the elimination of any one of them will necessarily lead to the elimination of the other two remain debated questions.

25. Marx, Engels, *Werke,* 20, p. 264 (English translation, Frederick Engels, *Anti-Dhring,* 2d ed. (Moscow: Foreign Languages Publishing House, 1959), p. 391).

26. See *Science and Ideology in Soviet Society,* pp. 67-81; A. F. Shishkin, "Problema sotsial'nogo determinizma i morali v rabotakh V. I. Lenina" [The Problem of Social Determinism and Morals in the Works of V. I. Lenin], *Voprosy filosofii,* 1967, 4, pp. 21-31.

27. Up through 1968 the following works on value theory appeared in the Soviet philosophical literature: A. F. Shishkin, "K voprosu o moral'nykh tsennostiakh" [Concerning the Question of Moral Values], *Doklady i vystupleniia predstaviteli sovetskoi nauki na XII mezhdunarodnom filosofskom kongresse* [*Papers and Addresses of the Soviet Delegates at the XII International Congress of Philosophy*] (Moskva: AN SSSR, 1958), 71-81; V. P. Tugarinov, *O tsennostiiakh zhizni i*

kul'tury; K. I. Gulian, "Marksistskaia etika i problema tsennosti" [Marxist Ethics and the Problem of Values], *Voprosy filosofii* 1962, 1, pp. 39-53 (though Gulian is a Rumanian his position is similar to that of the Soviets); I. F. Balakina, "Probleme tsennostei—vnimanie issledovatelei" [Pay Attention to Investigating the Problem of Values], *Voprosy filosofii* 1965, 9, pp. 152-59; A. P. Fedosova, "Poniatie tsennosti i marksistskaia etika" [The Concept of Value and Marxist Ethics], *Filosofskie nauki* 1965, 5, pp. 64-67; V. V. Mshvenieradze, "Marksizm i problema tsennostei" [Marxism and the Problem of Values], *Filosofskie nauki* 1965, 1, pp. 65-70; S. I. Popov, "Kategorii tsennosti i otsenki i marksistskaia filosofiia" [The Categories of Value and Valuation and Marxist Philosophy], *Filosofskie nauki* 1965, 5, pp. 55-63; A. F. Shishkin, "Chelovek kak vysshaia tsennost'" [Man as the Highest Value], *Voprosy filosofii* 1965, 1, pp. 3-15; I. F. Balakina, "Problema tsennosti i burzhuaznye aksiologicheskie ucheniia" [The Problem of Value and Bourgeois Axiological Teachings], *Filosofskie nauki* 1966, 3, pp. 75-82; O. I. Dzhioev, "Tsennost' i istoricheskaia neobkhodimost'" [Value and Historical Necessity], *Filosofskie nauki* 1966, 6, pp. 34-39; O. G. Drobnitskii, "Problema tsennosti i marksistskaia filosofiia" [The Problem of Value and Marxist Philosophy], *Voprosy filosofii* 1966, 7, pp. 33-44; O. M. Bakuradze, "Istina i tsennost'" [Truth and Value], *Voprosy filosofii* 1966, 7, pp. 45-48; A. F. Shishkin, "Sotsializm i moral'-nye tsennosti chelovechestva" [Socialism and the Moral Value of Mankind], *Voprosy filosofii* 1967, 10, pp. 64-75. For a fuller discussion of the Soviet position see Richard T. De George, "Value Theory in Soviet Philosophy: A Western Confrontation," *The Proceedings of the XIII International Congress of Philosophy*, IV, 1963, pp. 133-43.

Notes to Chapter III

1. L. M. Arkhangel'skii, *Kategorii marksistskoi etiki* [*Categories of Marxist Ethics*] (Moskva: Sotsekgiz, 1963), p. 8.

2. G. K. Gumnitskii, "K voprosy ob osnovnykh ethicheskikh kategoriiakh" [Concerning the Problem of the Basic Categories of Ethics], *Filosofskie nauki* 1963, 1, 127-32.

3. A. F. Shishkin, *Osnovy marksistskoi etiki*.

4. For a survey of the discussions see, A. G. Kharchev, "K itogam diskussii o kategoriiakh etiki" [Toward a Summation of the Discussion of Ethical Categories], *Filosofskie nauki* 1965, 2, 124-31.

5. L. M. Arkhangel'skii, "O sushchnosti eticheskikh kategorii" [On the Essence of Ethical Categories], *Filosofskie nauki* 1961, 3, 117-25.

6. Arkhangel'skii, op. cit., p. 58.

7. Ibid., pp. 7-57; Arkhangel'skii, art. cit.

8. V. P. Tugarinov, *O tsennostiakh zhizni i kul'tury*, p. 120.

9. Ibid., p. 121.

10. Gumnitskii, art. cit.

11. Arkhangel'skii, op. cit., p. 64.

12. See Tugarinov, op. cit., pp. 125-36.

13. Shishkin, op. cit., pp. 176-94.

14. L. M. Arkhangel'skii, "O kommunisticheskom nravstvennom ideale" [On the Communist Moral Ideal], *Voprosy filosofii* 1961, 11, 126-27.

15. Ibid., p. 128.

16. Part Two, Introduction. *The Road to Communism* (Moscow: Foreign Languages Publishing House), p. 509.

17. A. F. Shishkin, "Nevrazumitel'naia kritika" [An Unintelligible Criticism], *Voprosy filosofii* 1964, 5, p. 108.

18. *Osnovy marksistskoi filosofii,* izd. 2-e (Moskva: Izd. Pol. Lit., 1964), pp. 426-68.

19. Shishkin, art. cit., p. 111; A. F. Shishkin, "Sotsializm i moral'nye tsennosti chelovechestva," p. 64.

20. Ibid., p. 110.

21. V. V. Mshvenieradze, "Marksizm i problema tsennostei," p. 70.

22. I. F. Balakina, "Problema tsennostei—vnimanie issledovatelei," p. 157. V. P. Kobliakov, "Ob istinnosti moral'nykh suzhdenii" [On the Truth of Moral Judgments], *Voprosy filosofii* 1968, 5, 61-71, reviews a number of positions and concludes that though moral norms can be said to be true or false, the method of demonstrating their truth or falsity is complex and not the same as for simple descriptive sentences.

23. V. P. Tugarinov, *Lichnost' i obshchestvo* [*The Individual and Society*] (Moskva: "Mysl'", 1965), pp. 187-90. On the Soviet analysis of happiness see also, Arkhangel'skii, op. cit., Chapter IV; *Kategorii marksistsko-leninskoi etiki*, pp. 190-283; Shishkin, op. cit., pp. 417-27.

24. Tugarinov, *Lichnost' i obshchestvo*, pp. 185-86.

25. For a classical refutation see Eugen Böhm von Bawerk, *Karl Marx and the Close of His System*, ed. Paul M. Sweezy (New York: A. M. Kelley, 1949). This is a translation of Böhm von Bawerk's 1896 refutation of Marx's economic doctrine.

26. See *Voprosy filosofii* 1961, 11, 29-41; 1962, 10, 22-47; 1963, 3, 37-62; 1963, 9, 29-39; 1963, 11, 86-98; 1963, 12, 54-58; 1964, 1, 86-89; 1964, 6, 130-44.

27. T. I. Oiserman, "Man and His Alienation," *Philosophy, Science and Man: The Soviet Delegation Reports for the XIII World Congress of Philosophy* (Moscow: AN SSSR, 1963), pp. 99-107.

28. See, among others, Milovan Djilas, *The New Class* (New York and Washington: F. Praeger, 1957). For a bibliography of some non-Soviet writings on alienation see *Marxism & Alienation*, ed. Herbert Aptheker (New York: Humanities Press, 1965), pp. 152-58.

29. Shishkin, op. cit., pp. 194-99.

Notes to Chapter IV

1. *Osnovy marksistskoi filosofii*, p. 160; *Filosofskii slovar'*, pp. 363-64.

2. *Osnovy marksistskoi filosofii*, p. 161; *Filosofskii slovar'*, p. 121.

3. *Osnovy marksistskoi filosofii*, p. 166.

4. Ibid., pp. 166-67.

5. V. G. Ivanov, N. V. Rybakova, *Ocherki marksistsko-leninskoi etiki*, p. 142.

6. A. F. Shishkin, *Osnovy marksistskoi etiki*, p. 109.

7. See for instance Stalin's claims that the moral factor can play a role in the development of society, *Problems of Leninism* (Moscow: FLPH, 1954), p. 778.

8. See Richard T. De George, "Soviet Ethics and Soviet Society," *Studies in Soviet Thought,* IV (1964), pp. 206-17.

9. Among Soviet discussions of freedom see especially, D. A. Kerimov, "Svoboda i pravo" [Freedom and Law], *Filosofskie nauki* 1964, 3, 14-24; V. I. Mishin, "Kommunizm i svoboda" [Communism and Freedom], *Voprosy filosofii* 1965, 1, 146-53; A. P. Chermenina, "Ponimanie svobody v marksistsko-leninskoi etike" [The Conception of Freedom in Marxist-Leninist Ethics], *Filosofskie nauki* 1964, 6, 111-18; V. P. Tugarinov, *O tsennostiakh zhizni i kul'tury,* pp. 133-36; V. P. Tugarinov, *Lichnost' i obshchestvo,* pp. 61-66; Ivanov and Rybakova, op. cit., pp. 139-55.

10. S. Utkin, *Ocherki po marksistsko-leninskoi etike,* p. 111.

11. A. P. Chermenina, art. cit., p. 115.

12. Ivanov and Rybakova, op. cit., p. 147; Tugarinov, *O tsennostiakh zhizni i kul'tury,* p. 134; G. Smirnov, "Svoboda i otvetstvennost' lichnosti" [Freedom and Individual Responsibility], *Kommunist* 1966, 14, pp. 60-62.

13. Kerimov, art. cit., p. 14.

14. A. F. Shishkin, "Chelovek kak vysshaia tsennost' ", pp. 3-15.

15. Tugarinov, *O tsennostiakh zhizni i kul'tury,* p. 135.

16. Chermenina, art. cit., 115.

17. Ibid., p. 112.

18. Ibid., pp. 113-14.

19. Ibid., p. 118; Tugarinov, *Lichnost' i obschestvo,* p. 66; Mishin, art. cit., p. 146; Kermiov, art. cit., p. 21.

20. It is discussed in the following places: M. I. Mishin, "O moral'-noi otvetstvennosti kollektiva" [On the Moral Responsibility of a Collective], *Voprosy marksistsko-leninskoi etiki* [*Problems of Marxist-Leninist Ethics*] (Moskva: Gosudarstvennoe izd. politicheskoi literatury, 1960), pp. 93-101; E. G. Fedorenko, *Osnovy marksistsko-leninskoi etiki,* pp. 125 ff.; A. P. Chermenina, "Problema otvetstvennosti v sovremen-noi burzhyaznoi etiki" [The Problem of Responsibility in Contempo-rary Bourgeois Ethics], *Voprosy filosofii* 1965, 2, 76-87; Tugarinov, *O tsennostiakh zhizni i kul'tury,* pp. 132-33; Tugarinov, *Lichnost' i*

obshchestvo, pp. 52 ff.; Shishkin, op. cit., pp. 204-9; Ivanov and Rybakova, op. cit., p. 147, *Osnovy marksistsko-leninskoi etiki* [Fundamentals of Marxist-Leninist Ethics] (Minsk: Vysshaia Shkola, 1965), pp. 55-57; Smirnov, art. cit.

21. Tugarinov, *Lichnost'i obshchestvo*, p. 52; Ivanov and Rybakova, op. cit., p. 147.

22. Tugarinov, *O tsennostiakh zhizni i kul'tury*, p. 133.

23. Idem.

24. Ivanov and Rybakova, p. 155.

25. Ibid. pp. 146 ff.

26. See below, pp. 77-80.

27. *Osnovy marksistsko-leninskoi etiki*, p. 56; Chermenina, "Ponimanie svobody v marksistsko-leninskoi etike," p. 112.

28. A. F. Shishkin, "Nekotorye voprosy teorii kommunisticheskoi morali," *Voprosy filosofii* 1956, 4, 3-17.

29. Mishin, "O moral'noi otvetsvennosti kollektiva," p. 95.

30. Idem; Smirnov, art. cit., p. 68.

31. Mishin, p. 98.

32. O. G. Drobnitskii, "K voprosu o kategorii dolga v marksistskoi etike" [On the Question of the Category of Duty in Marxist Ethics], *Filosofskie nauki* 1960, 3, pp. 111-12.

33. Ibid. pp. 112-13.

34. *Osnovy marksistsko-leninskoi etiki*, p. 69; L. M. Arkhangel'skii, *Kategorii marksistskoi etiki*, op. cit., p. 91; Fedorenko, op. cit., 147.

35. L. M. Arkhangel'skii, "Dobro, dolg, sovest'" [Good, Duty, Conscience], *Voprosy filosofii* 1964, 6, 75; Drobnitskii, art. cit., pp. 110-11; I. V. Konovalova, "Dolg kak kategoriia marksistsko-leninskoi etiki" [Duty as a Category of Marxist-Leninist Ethics], *Problemy etiki* [*Problems of Ethics*] (Moskva: Izd. "Nauka," 1964), p. 32.

36. Konovalova, art. cit., p. 38.

37. Fedorenko, op. cit., p. 152; *Filosofskii slovar'*, p. 137.

38. L. M. Arkhangel'skii, "O sushchnosti eticheskikh categorii," *Filosofskie nauki* 1961, 3, pp. 117-25.

39. Konovalova, art. cit., p. 39.

40. G. K. Gumnitskii, art. cit., pp. 127-32.

41. Shishkin, op. cit., pp. 428-38.

42. Arkhangel'skii, "Dobro, dolg, sovest'," p. 76.

43. Tugarinov, *O tsennostiakh zhizni i kul'tury*, pp. 120-21.

44. Arkhangel'skii, op. cit., pp. 11-16. P. E. Filonovich, *O Kommunisticheskoi morali* [On Communist Morals] (Moskva: Politizdat, 1963), p. 137; Utkin, op. cit., p. 292; Fedorenko, op. cit., p. 165; I. I. Rezvitskii, "O sushchnosti kategorii sovesti" [On the Essence of the Category of Conscience], *Filosofskie nauki* 1967, 2, p. 65.

45. Z. A. Berbeshkina, *Problema sovesti v marksistsko-leninskoi etike* [The Problem of Conscience in Marxist-Leninist Ethics] (Moskva: Izd. Vysshei Partiinoi Shkoly i Akad. Obshchestvennykh Nauk pri Tsk KPSS, 1963), pp. 22, 71.

46. Shishkin, op. cit., pp. 410-13; *Filosofskii slovar'*, p. 409.

47. *Kategorii marksistsko-leninskoi etiki* [Categories of Marxist-Leninist Ethics] (Moskva: Izd. "Mysl'," 1965), p. 90.

48. L. B. Volchenko, "Marksistsko-leninskaia etika o sovesti" [Marxist-Leninist Ethics on Conscience], *Voprosy filosofii* 1962, 2, 134-35; Arkhangel'skii, op. cit., p. 170.

49. *Kategorii marksistsko-leninskoi etiki*, p. 45.

50. Fedorenko, op. cit., p. 175.

51. Shishkin, op. cit., p. 512; A. F. Shishkin, *Osnovy kommunisticheskoi morali* [Foundations of Communist Morals] (Moskva: Gosudarstvennoe Izd. Politicheskoi Literatury, 1955), chap. IV.

52. The following constitute the bulk of the discussions: Tugarinov, *O tsennostiakh zhizni i kul'tury*, pp. 130-31; Shishkin, *Osnovy marksistskoi etiki*, pp. 204-9; A. F. Shishkin, "Nekotorye voprosy teorii kommunisticheskoi morali" [Some Problems in the Theory of Communist Morals], *Voprosy filosofii* 1956, 4, pp. 7-8; *Osnovy marksistsko-leninskoi etiki*, pp. 57-60; N. N. Mokrousov, "Problema nravstvennoi

otsenki postupkov (povedeniia) " [The Problem of the Moral Valuation of Conduct (Behavior)], *Voprosy filosofii* 1965, 9, 37-46.

53. Shishkin, "Nekotorye voprosy teorii kommunisticheskoi morali," p. 7 quotes Lenin in defense of this view; in his *Osnovy marksistskoi etiki* Shishkin refers to Marx in support of the position (pp. 205-7).

54. On this point see George L. Kline, "Economic Crime and Punishment," *Survey*, No. 57 (October 1965), pp. 67-72.

55. Tugarinov mentions human rights in *O tsennostiakh zhizni i kul'tury* (p. 41) but he does not develop the notion; Ivanov and Rybakova, op. cit., p. 203, mention the right to work, rest, education, and social security, but without development or clarification as to what kind of rights these are.

56. See for example, Arkhangel'skii, op. cit., 65-68; *Osnovy marksistsko-leninskoi etiki*, pp. 66-68; Ivanov and Rybakova, op. cit. pp. 194-205; Fedorenko, op. cit., p. 141; V. S. Pazenok, *Sotsializm i spravidlivost'* [*Socialism and Justice*], Moskva: Izdatel'stvo "Mysl'," 1967.

57. Arkhangel'skii, op. cit., p. 67; *Osnovy marksistsko-leninskoi etiki*, pp. 66-68.

58. *Osnovy marksistsko-leninskoi etiki*, p. 68.

59. Tugarinov, *O tsennostiakh zhizni i kul'tury*, pp. 82-83; Fedorenko, op. cit., p. 141.

Notes to Chapter v

1. Programme of the Communist Party of the Soviet Union, Part Two, V, 1 (*The Road to Communism: Documents of the 22nd Congress of the Communist Party of the Soviet Union*, Moscow: Foreign Languages Publishing House, pp. 566-67). The Party Program was closely tied to N. Khrushchev. But though the Program has been played down since 1965 the principles of the moral code have not been so treated and still form part of the course outlines for instruction in the institutions of higher education and of the presently used textbooks. The principles continue to be discussed in the Soviet ethical literature. *Kratkii slovar' po filosofii* [*Short Dictionary of Philosophy*] (Moskva: Izdatel'stvo Politicheskoi Literatury, 1966) lists the same moral prin-

ciples as the 1961 Program, as does *Moral'nyi oblik sovetskogo rabochego* [*The Moral Make-up of the Soviet Worker*] (Moskva: Mockovskii rabochii, 1966). In the 1963 edition of *Moral' kak ee ponimaiut kommunisty* [*Morality As Communists Understand It*] (Moskva: Gosudarstvennoe izdatel'stvo politicheskoi literatury) the moral code is included in section 3 and statements by Khrushchev are reprinted in section 8. In the 1966 edition of the same book section 8 has been completely deleted but section 3 remains, including the entire moral code verbatim. The moral principles enunciated in the code were discussed in Soviet philosophical writings before Khrushchev came to power and have continued to be discussed after his fall from power.

2. *Nravstvennye printsipy stroitelia kommunizma* [*Moral Principles of the Builder of Communism*] (Moskva: Izd. "Mysl'," 1965), p. 7.

3. Ibid., p. 5.

4. Ibid., p. 16.

5. Ibid., p. 7; on the active role of the superstructure see Richard T. De George, *Patterns of Soviet Thought,* Ann Arbor: The University of Michigan Press, 1966, 189-90, 194-98.

6. *Nravstvennye printsipy stroitelia kommunizma,* p. 6.

7. S. Utkin, *Ocherki po marksistsko-leninskoi etike,* p. 169.

8. *The Road to Communism,* p. 599.

9. *Nravstvennye printsipy stroitelia kommunizma,* p. 56.

10. A. F. Shishkin, *Osnovy marksistskoi etiki,* p. 7 fn.

11. *The Road to Communism,* p. 566.

12. Idem.

13. I. Kuz'minkov, "Kommunisticheskaia moral' i obshchecheloveche-cheskie normy nravstvennosti," pp. 88-91.

14. *Nravstvennye printsipy stroitelia kommunizma,* p. 17.

15. Ibid., p. 20.

16. Ibid., p. 21.

17. See Chapter III.

18. *Nravstvennye printsipy stroitelia kommunizma,* p. 47; Utkin, op. cit., p. 172; see also "Patriotizm i internatsionalizm sovetskogo naroda" [The Patriotism and Internationalism of the Soviet People], *Kommunist* 1966, 9, pp. 3-11.

19. Shishkin, op. cit., p. 232.

20. *Karl Marx, Friedrich Engels, Werke* (Berlin: Dietz Verlag), 3, p. 21 (English translation, Karl Marx and Friedrich Engels, *The German Ideology* (N.Y.: International Publishers, 1967), p. 7.

21. *Marx-Engels Werke,* 20, p. 444 (Engels, "The Part Played by Labour in the Transition from Ape to Man").

22. Shishkin, op. cit., p. 286; *Nravstvennye printsipy stroitelia kommunizma,* p. 86.

23. The needs of the people are to be "rationally determined" by the leaders of the Party.

24. Cf. George Fischer, *Science and Politics: The New Sociology in the Soviet Union* (Ithaca: Cornell University, 1964), chap. IV, where Fischer speaks of the Soviet "sociology of work."

25. Shishkin, op. cit., p. 307; see the ninth principle of the moral code of the builder of communism.

26. Propagandists for the Soviet Union make much of its woman cosmonaut, as well as of the fact that there are more female than male doctors. Women perform manual labor of most sorts, though they are no longer allowed to work in the coal mines.

27. *Nravstvennye printsipy stroitelia kommunizma,* pp. 71-72.

28. Shishkin, op. cit., pp. 296-306.

29. *Osnovy marksistsko-leninskoi etiki* (Minsk), p. 118; *Nravstvennye printsipy stroitelia kommunizma,* pp. 138-39. Soviet philosophers do not distinguish between egoism and individualism though the two are by no means identical.

30. See pp. 14-15, 29-33, 46-51.

31. *Nravstvennye printsipy stroitelia kommunizma,* p. 140.

32. Shishkin, op. cit., pp. 229-31.

33. Ibid., pp. 250-52; *Nravstvennye printsipy stroitelia kommunizma*, pp. 137-50.

34. Shishkin, op. cit., pp. 236-40, 250.

35. See Richard T. De George, "A Bibliography of Soviet Ethics," *Studies in Soviet Thought*, III (1963), pp. 83-103.

36. Shishkin, op. cit., p. 252.

37. Ibid., p. 276.

38. Ibid., p. 320; *Nravstvennye printsipy stroitelia kommunizma*, p. 277.

39. Shishkin, op. cit., p. 324.

40. *Nravstvennye printsipy stroitelia kommunizma*, p. 190.

41. Ibid., pp. 210-36.

42. Part II of the *Manifesto* (Karl Marx and Frederick Engels, *Selected Works in Two Volumes* (Moscow: Foreign Languages Publishing House, 1958), vol. I, pp. 50-51).

43. See especially Alexandra Kollontai, *Communism and the Family* (New York, 1920). A few pertinent pages of this work are reprinted in Thornton Anderson (ed.), *Masters of Russian Communism* (New York: Appleton-Century-Crofts, 1963), pp. 175-78.

44. *Communist Morality* (Moscow: Progress Publishers), pp. 70-71.

45. For a more detailed account of the history of the Soviet family and the laws surrounding it, see A. G. Kharchev, *Brak i sem'ja v SSSR* [Marriage and the Family in the USSR] (Moskva: "Mysl'," 1964); also, E. W. Burgess and H. J. Locke, *The Family* (N.Y.: American Book Co., 2d ed., 1953), Chapter 6; Harold J. Berman, *Justice in the U. S. S. R.,* revised ed. (New York: Vintage Books, 1963), Chapter 14.

46. V. Chekalin, *Liubov' i sem'ia* [*Love and the Family*] (Moskva: Izd. Politicheskoi Literatury, 1964), pp. 71-73; Iu. A. Korolev, "Sootnoshenie morali i prava v brachno-semeinykh otnosheniiakh" [The Correlation of Morality and Law in the Regulation of Marriage and Family Life], *Voprosy filosofii* 1963, 11, pp. 78-81.

47. Chekalin, op. cit., pp. 71-73.

48. *Osnovy marksistsko-leninskoi etiki* (Minsk), p. 159. There is hardly any discussion in the Soviet ethical literature about questions of homosexuality or other specific aspects of sexual morality. Legal statutes are a much more explicit source of what is considered illegal (and so immoral) and socially harmful. See *Soviet Criminal Law and Procedure: The RSFSR Codes,* trans. Harold J. Berman and James W. Spindler (Cambridge, Mass.: Harvard University Press, 1966).

49. See F. B. Sadykov, "Novyi nauchnyi trud po marksistskoi etike" [A New Scientific Work on Marxist Ethics], *Filosofskie nauki* 1962, 6, pp. 95-96. I. S. Kon, "Tsennoe issledovanie" [A Valuable Study], *Filosofskie nauki* 1965, 1, p. 122, complains that the typical Soviet works on marriage and the family pay little attention to the sexual-psychological aspects of these; Chekalin, op. cit., p. 79 blandly claims that marriage for love is the solution of the sex problem for most young people, though sometimes problems (which are not discussed) still remain.

50. *Osnovy marksistsko-leninskoi etiki* (Minsk), p. 158; E. G. Fedorenko, *Osnovy marksistsko-leninskoi etiki* (Kiev: Izd. Kievskogo Un-ta, 1965), p. 268; *Nravstvennye printsipy stroitelia kommunizma,* p. 212.

51. *The Road to Communism,* pp. 544-45.

52. Ibid., p. 544: "By virtue of all this public catering will be able to take precedence over home cooking within 10-15 years."

53. See pp. 43-44, 53-54.

54. Though I hope the paternalistic parallel is enlightening, it should not be pushed too far. The Party remains an institution, it can administer capital punishment, and it is not restrained by any laws not of its own making.

55. See Shishkin, op. cit., pp. 176-82; V. P. Tugarinov, "Kommunizm i lichnost'" [Communism and the Individual], *Voprosy filosofii* 1962, 6, p. 16.

Notes to Chapter VI

1. Adam Schaff, *A Philosophy of Man* (New York: The Monthly Review Press, 1963), p. 83.

2. *The Road to Communism: Documents of the 22nd Congress of the Communist Party of the Soviet Union* (Moscow: Foreign Languages Publishing House), pp. 565-66.

3. "Current Tasks of the Party's Ideological Work," delivered June 18, 1963. It appeared in *Pravda*, June 19, 1963, and in English translation in *Current Digest of the Soviet Press,* July 3, 1963. This quote is from p. 10 of the English translation.

4. *The Road to Communism,* p. 509.

5. L. B. Volchenko, "Marksistsko-leninskaia etika o sovesti," p. 134; "Obshchestvennyi dolg sovestskogo cheloveka" [The Social Duty of Soviet Man], *Kommunist,* 1965, 2, pp. 6-9; *23rd Congress of the Communist Party of the Soviet Union,* (Moscow: Novesti Press, 1966), p. 148.

6. M. S. Danielian, *Nekotorye voprosy marksistsko-leninskoi etiki* [*Some Problems of Marxist-Leninist Ethics*] (Erevan: Izd. AN Armianskoi SSR, 1962), 40-54; *Voprosy teorii i praktiki kommunisticheskogo vospitaniia* [*Problems of Theory and Practice in Communist Education*] (Moskva: Izd. VPSh i AON, 1962), p. 26; A. F. Shishkin, *Osnovy marksistskoi etiki,* pp. 115-22.

7. See Iu. A. Korolev, "Sootnoshenie morali i prava v brachno-semeinykh otnosheniiakh," pp. 79-85; T. I. Nikolaeva, "Sootnoshenie sotsialisticheskogo prava i morali i pererastanie ikh v normy kommunisticheskogo obshchezhitiia" [The Correlation of Socialist Law and Morality and Their Development into Norms of Communist Society], *Voprosy gosudarstva i prava* [*Problems of the State and of Law*] (Leningrad: Izd. Leningradskogo Universiteta, 1964), pp. 96-101.

8. Danielian, op. cit., pp. 53-54; N. A. Trofimov, "O perspektivakh razvitiia morali i prava v ikh vzaimnom otnoshenii" [On the Prospects of the Development of Morality and Law in Their Mutual Relations], *Voprosy filosofii,* 1962, 5, pp. 24-26; Korolev, art. cit., p. 79; *Voprosy gosudarstva i prava,* p. 98.

9. See for instance, *Communist Morality* (Moscow: Progress Publishers), pp. 195-96, and *The Road to Communism,* p. 118.

10. See Harold J. Berman and James W. Spindler, "Soviet Comrades' Courts," *Washington Law Review,* Vol. 38 (1963), pp. 842-910, for both the 1961 RSFSR Statute on comrades' courts and a commentary on and analysis of it.

11. See B. Z. Boziev's article on Party morality and its role in strengthening the Party in conditions of building communism, *Voprosy marksistsko-leninskoi etiki* [Problems of Marxist-Leninist Ethics] (Moskva: Izd. VPSh i AON pri Tsk KPSS, 1962), pp. 129-63; *Voprosy teorii i praktiki kommunisticheskogo, vospitanie*, p. 27.

12. *O kommunisticheskoi etike*, p. 334.

13. See, for example, *Kommunisticheskaia moral'i voinskii dolg* [*Communist Morality and Military Duty*] (Moskva: Voenizdat, 1960), which is a collection of articles on communist morality and military duty.

14. M. I. Kalinin, *On Communist Education* (Moscow: Foreign Languages Publishing House, 1950), p. 445.

15. *Kommunisticheskaia moral'i voinskii dolg*, p. 44.

16. Ibid., p. 46.

17. Ibid., p. 67.

18. G. G. Filippov, "O roli moral'nogo faktora v sovremennom promyshlennom proizvodstve" [On the Role of the Moral Factor in Contemporary Industrial Production], *Filosofskie nauki* 1965, 5, pp. 47-51. See also Iu. I. Palkin, "Sochetanie material'nykh i moral'nykh stimulov k trudu pri sotsializme" [The Combination of Material and Moral Incentives to Work Under Socialism], *Voprosy filosofii* 1966, 6, pp. 3-13.

19. N. F. Naumova, "Dva mira—dva otnosheniia k trudu" [Two Worlds: Two Attitudes Toward Labor], *Voprosy filosofii* 1963, 1, p. 23; M. N. Laptin, *V. I. Lenin o material'nykh i moral'nykh stimulakh k trudu* [*V. I. Lenin on Material and Moral Incentives to Work*] (Moskva: Ekonomizdat, 1962), pp. 145-47.

20. Laptin, op. cit., p. 147; N. N. Mokrousov, "Trudovaia deiatel'nost' kollektiva i voprosy nravstvennogo vospitaniia" [The Working Activity of a Collective and the Problems of Moral Education], *Voprosy filosofii* 1963, 10, p. 50; F. Petrenko i G. Khrustev, "Chelovek budushchego formiruetsia segodnia" [The Man of the Future Is Being Formed Today], *Kommunist* 1962, 17, p. 48.

21. Laptin, op. cit., p. 154.

22. Petrenko i Khrustev, art. cit., p. 47.

23. Naumova, art. cit., p. 23.

24. M. G. Zhuravkov, "XXII S"ezd KPSS i nekotorye voprosy etiki" [The 22nd Congress of the CPSU and Some Problems of Ethics], *Voprosy filosofii* 1962, 2, p. 9; *Communist Morality*, p. 201.

25. *The Road to Communism*, p. 566.

26. Ibid., p. 583.

27. A. I. Goriacheva, "O vzaimootnoshenii ideologii i obshchestvennoi psikhologii" [The Interrelation Between Ideology and Social Psychology], *Voprosy filosofii* 1963, 11, pp. 57-65; V. N. Kolbanovskii, "Nekotorye aktual'nye problemy obshchestvennoi psikhologii" [Some Pressing Problems of Social Psychology], *Voprosy filosofii* 1963, 12, pp. 16-25.

28. Volchenko, art. cit., p. 134.

29. *O kommunisticheskoi etike,* pp. 399-400; Kolbanovskii, art. cit., pp. 19-23.

30. Volchenko, art. cit., p. 144.

31. *O kommunisticheskoi etike,* pp. 37, 380-81; *Osnovy marksistsko-leninskoi etiki* (Minsk), p. 207; N. I. Boldyrev, *Vospitanie kommunisticheskoi morali u shkol'nikov* [The Inculcation of Communist Morality in Schoolboys], izd. 2 (Moskva: Gosudarstvennoe Uchebno-pedagogicheskoe Izdatelstvo Ministerstva Prosveshcheniia RSFSR, 1956), pp. 42 ff; L. Tolkunov, "Problemy nravstvennogo vospitaniia i pechat'" [Problems of Moral Education and the Press], *Kommunist* 1967, 2, 73-84.

32. Boldyrev, op. cit., p. 23.

33. *Voprosy marksistsko-leninskoi etiki* (Moskva, 1960), p. 54.

34. *Communist Morality*, pp. 195-96.

35. See for instance *Osnovy kommunisticheskogo vospitaniia* [*Fundamentals of Communist Education*], 2 izd. (Moskva: Gospolitizdat, 1962), Chapter 8.

36. *Osnovy marksistsko-leninskoi etiki*, p. 207.

37. Boldyrev, op. cit., pp. 162 ff.

38. *Osnovy marksistsko-leninskoi etiki*, p. 206; V. G. Ivanov, N. V. Rybakova, *Ocherki marksistsko-leninskoi etiki*, p. 222; E. G. Fedorenko, *Osnovy marksistsko-leninskoi etiki*, p. 288. It is also Makarenko (1883-1939) and not Pavlov who is frequently quoted in *Marksistskaia etika: Khrestomatiia [Marxist Ethics: A Reader]* (Moskva: Izd. In-t. Mezhdunarodnykh Otnoshenii, 1961).

39. Ivanov and Rybakova, op. cit., p. 222; Kolbanovskii, art cit., p. 23.

40. Fedorenko, op. cit., pp. 285, 288; *Communist Morality*, p. 85; G. Smirnov, "Svoboda i otvetstvennost' lichnosti," p. 68.

41. For the analogous parental aspect of Soviet law, see Berman, *Justice in the U.S.S.R.*, Part III.

42. See, for example, I. M. Popova, "Teorii sotsial'nogo kontrolia v amerikanskoi sotsiologii" [Theories of Social Control in American Sociology], *Voprosy filosofii* 1965, 6, pp. 104-12.

Notes to Chapter VII

1. K. A. Shvartsman, *Etika bez morali: Kritika sovremennykh burzhuaznykh eticheskikh teorii [Ethics Without Morality: A Critique of Contemporary Bourgeois Ethical Theories]* (Moskva: Izd. "Mysl'," 1964), p. 4.

2. See Ibid., p. 5; also K. A. Shvartsman, "O nravstvennom sostoianii i etike sovremennogo burzhuaznogo obshchestva" [On the Moral Condition and the Ethics of Contemporary Bourgeois Society], *Problemy etiki [Problems of Ethics]* (Moskva: "Nauka," 1964), p. 162-63; E. G. Fedorenko, *Osnovy marksistsko-leninskoi etiki*, p. 295; *Kritika ideologii antikommunizma [A Critique of the Ideology of Anticommunism]* (Moskva: Izd. Vysshaia Shkola, 1965), pp. 257-65.

3. See Part I, section IV.

4. See above, Chapter IV.

5. E.g., *Programa kursa "Osnovy marksistsko-leninskoi etiki" dlia vysshikh uchebnykh zavedenii [Syllabus of the Course "Fundamentals of Marxist-Leninist Ethics" for Higher Educational Institutions]*, izd. 3 (Moskva: Gosudarstvennoe Izd. Politicheskoi Literatury, 1962) p. 17; *Primernyi uchebnotematicheskii plan i programma po osnovam marksistsko-leninskoi etiki [A Model Curriculum and Program for Funda-*

mentals of Marxist-Leninist Ethics] (Moskva: Izd. "Znanie" 1962), p. 20; *Osnovy marksistsko-leninskoi etiki* (Minsk), p. 212.

6. M. Koval'zon, "Mirovozzrenie i moral'" [World View and Morals], *Kommunist* 1962, 17, p. 39; A. F. Shishkin, *Osnovy marksistskoi etiki*, pp. 79-89.

7. Shvartsman, art. cit., pp. 163-67.

8. *Kritika ideologii antikommunizma,* p. 265.

9. R. C. Angell, *Free Society and Moral Crisis* (Ann Arbor: University of Michigan Press, 1965), p. 8.

10. Ibid., p. 12.

11. This is the way Angell defines low integration (p. 8).

12. Angell, op. cit., p. 20.

13. Fedorenko, op. cit., p. 295.

14. D. V. Ermolenko, *Kritika sovremennoi burzhuaznoi filosofii* [*A Critique of Contemporary Bourgeois Philosophy*] (Moskva: Gosudarstvennoe Izd. Vysshaia Shkola, 1959), p. 24 ff.

15. *Protiv sovremennoi burzhuaznoi filosofii* [*Against Contemporary Bourgeois Philosophy*] (Moskva: Izd. Moskovskogo Universiteta, 1963), pp. 111-12.

16. *Programa kursa. . . ,* p. 17.

17. Shvartsman, art. cit., p. 117.

18. Fedorenko, op. cit., p. 296.

19. Shvartsman, art. cit., p. 181; Shvartsman, op. cit., p. 36.

20. *Osnovy marksistsko-leninskoi etiki,* p. 213.

21. Ibid., p. 214.

22. Idem; *Programa kursa. . . ,* p. 17; *Voprosy marksistsko-leninskoi etiki* (Moskva: Gospolitizdat, 1960) p. 224.

23. *Programa kursa. . . ,* p. 17; *Voprosy marksistsko-leninskoi etiki,* p. 224; Fedorenko, op. cit., p. 299.

24. *Osnovy marksistsko-leninskoi etiki,* p. 217; *Voprosy marksistskoleninskoi etiki,* p. 224; Shvartsman, art. cit., p. 181.

25. *Protiv sovremennoi burzhuaznoi filosofii*, p. 112; *Programa kursa. . .* , p. 17; *Voprosy marksistsko-leninskoi etiki*, pp. 225-26.

26. *Osnovy marksistsko-leninskoi etiki*, pp. 225.

27. *Programa kursa . . .* , p. 17.

28. Idem; *Osnovy marksistsko-leninskoi etiki*, pp. 217-18.

29. *Programa kursa . . .* , p. 18; *Osnovy marksistsko-leninskoi etiki*, p. 229.

30. *Programa kursa . . .* , p. 18; *Osnovy marksistsko-leninskoi etiki*, p. 236.

31. V. I. Lenin, *Polnoe sobranie sochinenii*, vol. 29, p. 161. For English translation see V. I. Lenin, *Collected Works*, vol. 38, p. 179.

32. See the article cited in Chapter IV, note 54, above.

33. The nature of morality is presently a central topic of discussion among many Western philosophers. See William K. Frankena, "Recent Conceptions of Morality," *Morality and the Language of Conduct*, ed. Hector-Neri Castaneda and George Nakhnikian (Detroit: Wayne State University Press, 1965) .

34. For specific references, see my article "Morality, Ethics and East-European Marxism," *Inquiry*, Vol. 9 (1966) , pp. 24-27.

Bibliography

A. *Selected Bibliography of Works on Soviet and Marxist Ethics in Languages Other Than Russian.*

Acton, H. B. *The Illusion of the Epoch: Marxism-Leninism as a Philosophical Creed.* London: Cohen & West, 1955. Part II, Chapter II: "Marxist Ethics."

Ash, William. *Marxism and Moral Concepts.* New York: Monthly Review Press, 1964.

Bigo, Pierre. *Marxisme et humanisme.* Paris: Presses Universitaires de France, 1953.

Boeck, Hans. *Zur marxistischen Ethik und socialistischen Moral.* Berlin: Akademie-Verlag, 1959.

Cameron, J. M. *A Scrutiny of Marxism.* London: SCM Press, 1948.

Carew Hunt, R. N. *The Theory and Practice of Communism: An Introduction.* London: Geoffrey Bles, 1950. Chapter VII: "The Marxist Ethic."

Chambre, H. *Le marxisme en Union Sovietique: Ideologie et institutions, leurs évolution de 1917 à nos jours.* Paris: Editions du Seuil, 1955.

De George, Richard T. "A Bibliography of Soviet Ethics," *Studies in Soviet Thought,* III (1963), pp. 83-103.

_____. "The Foundations of Marxist-Leninist Ethics," *Studies in Soviet Thought,* III (1963), pp. 121-33.

_____. "Morality, Ethics, and East European Marxism," *Inquiry,* IX (1966), pp. 11-29.

_____. "Soviet Ethics and Soviet Society," *Studies in Soviet Thought,* IV (1964), pp. 206-17.

Garaudy, Roger. *Qu'est-ce que la morale marxiste?* Paris: Éditions sociales, 1963.

175

Hodges, Donald C. "Historical Materialism in Ethics," *Philosophy and Phenomenological Research*, XXIII (1962-63), pp. 1-22.

Kamenka, Eugene. *The Ethical Foundations of Marxism*. London: Routledge and Kegan Paul; New York: Praeger, 1962.

Kautsky, Karl. *Ethics and the Materialist Conception of History*. Chicago: Charles H. Kerr & Company, 1907.

Kline, George L. "Leszek Kolakowski and the Revision of Marxism," *European Philosophy Today*, ed. George L. Kline. Chicago: Quadrangle Books, 1965.

————. " 'Socialist Legality' and Communist Ethics," *Natural Law Forum*, VIII (1963), pp. 21-34.

Kramer, Richard. *Practical Morality Taught to Soviet Children, as Illustrated in Four Official Soviet Periodicals, 1937-1951*. Ann Arbor: University Microfilms, 1954.

Marcuse, Herbert. *Soviet Marxism: A Critical Analysis*. New York: Vintage Books, 1961. Part II: "Ethical Tenets."

Marković, Mihailo. "Marxist Humanism and Ethics," *Inquiry*, VI (1963), pp. 18-34.

Parsons, Howard L. *Ethics in the Soviet Union Today*. New York: American Institute for Marxist Studies, 1965.

Pennati, Eugenio. *L'etica e il marxismo*. Firenze: La Nuova Italia, 1948.

Peterffy, Gedeone. "The Ethics of Communism," *The Philosophy of Communism*. New York: Fordham University Press, 1949.

Popper, Karl R. *The Open Society and Its Enemies*. 4th ed. (revised). London: Routledge and Kegan Paul, 1962. Vol. II, Chapter 22: "The Moral Theory of Historicism."

Rubel, Maximilien. *Pages choisies pour une éthique socialiste*. Paris: Librairie Marcel Rivière et Cie., 1948.

Selsam, Howard. *Ethics and Progress*. New York: International Publishers, 1965.

————. *Socialism and Ethics*. New York: International Publishers, 1943.

Trotskii, Lev D. *Their Morals and Ours*. New York: Pioneer Publishers, 1942.

B. *Selected Bibliography of Works in Russian.*

A complete bibliography of Soviet writings on ethics and morality from 1924 through the middle of 1968 would include 600 items. Of these only three books and twenty-five articles appeared before 1947. For a listing and analysis of the Soviet ethical literature between 1947 and October 1962, see my bibliography cited in the preceding section. Articles and books on ethics and morality have continued to flow from the Soviet presses at a sustained rate since 1962, indicating no abatement in interest in these areas. The major topics of discussion during the last five years are similar to those of the previous five years. More books and articles are devoted to communist morality and its inculcation than to any other topic; critiques of Western ethical theories form the second largest group. The importance of labor for the good of society continues to be underlined; the discussion of ethical categories remains the focus of those interested in the technical questions of ethics; and value theory and humanism continue to be topics of interest.

Of the 338 Soviet authors of works on ethics or morality, only fourteen have written more than three items. Of these A. F. Shishkin is the most prolific, though conservative and unimaginative. A. G. Kharchev is the most important writer on questions of the family and marriage. O. G. Drobnitskii and K. A. Shvartsman are the most knowledgeable and well-informed critics of Anglo-American ethical writings; L. M. Arkhangel'skii is the leader in the Soviet discussions on ethical categories. V. P. Tugarinov has led the recent development of Soviet interest in value theory.

The works cited in the text and notes of this book are among the most influential and representative of the professional Soviet literature on ethics and morality. The works listed in the following bibliography form a supplement to those and will give the reader a further idea of this literature.

Aktual'nye problemy marksistskoi etiki [*Pressing Problems of Marxist Ethics*]. Sb. statei. Tbilisi, 1967. 495 pp.

Arkhangel'skii, L. M. "Obshchestvennyi dolg stroitelia kommunizma" [The Social Duty of the Builder of Communism], *Kommunist* 1963, 3, 46-53.

Drobnitskii, O. G. "Moral'naia degradatsiia kapitalizma" [The Moral Degradation of Capitalism], *Kommunist* 1963, 8, 113-20.

Drobnitskii, O. G., Kuz'mina, T. A. *Kritika sovremennykh burzhuaznykh eticheskikh kontsepii* [*A Critique of Contemporary Bourgeois Ethical Views*]. Moskva: "Vysshaia Shkola", 1967. 383 pp.

Dukhovnoe razvitie lichnosti [*The Spiritual Development of the Individual*]. Sverdlovsk, 1967. 332 pp.

Gumnitskii, G. K. "Smysl zhizni, schast'e, moral' " [The Meaning of Life, Happiness, Morality], *Voprosy filosofii* 1967, 5, 102-5.

Iovchuk, M. T. "Problema dukhovnoi svobody v sotsialisticheskom obshchestve" [The Problem of Spiritual Freedom in Socialist Society], *Filosofskie nauki* 1966, 2, 22-33.

Ivin, A. A. "Deonticheskaia logika" [Deontic Logic], *Voprosy filosofii* 1966, 12, 160-71.

Kedrov, B. M. "O determinizme" [On Determinism], *Filosofskie nauki* 1968, 1, 41-48.

Kharchev, A. G. "Byt i sem'ia pri sotsializme" [The Mode of Life and the Family Under Socialism], *Voprosy filosofii* 1967, 3, 12-19.

————. "Moral' kak predmet sotsiologicheskogo issledovaniia" [Morals as a Subject of Sociological Research], *Voprosy filosofii* 1965, 1, 45-55.

————. "XXIII S"ezd KPSS i nekotorye problemy kommunisticheskogo vospitaniia" [The XXIII Congress of the CPSU and Some Problems of Communist Education], *Filosofskie nauki* 1967, 2, 3-13.

Kissel', M. A. i Emdin, M. V. *Etika Gegelia i krizis sovremennoi burzhuaznoi etiki* [*Hegel's Ethics and the Crisis of Contemporary Bourgeois Ethics*]. Leningrad: Izd. LGU, 1966. 124 pp.

Kolbanovskii, V. N. "Moral'nyi kodeks stroitelia kommunizma" [The Moral Code of the Builder of Communism], *Kommunist* 1961, 15, 36-46.

Moral'nyi kodeks stroitelia kommunizma [The Moral Code of the Builder of Communism]. Obshchaia red. A. S. Vishniakova, M. G. Zhuravkova. Izd. 2-e. Moskva: Politizdat, 1965. 176 pp.

Ponomarev, V. *Stimul material'nyi i stimul moral'nyi (k trudu)* [Material and Moral Incentives to Work]. Alma-Ata: "Kazakhstan," 1965. 151 pp.

Problemy nravstvennogo formirovaniia lichnosti [*Problems of the Moral Formation of the Individual*]. Red. D. I. Chesnokov. Moskva: Moskovskii Universitet, 1967. 266 pp.

Publichnaia Biblioteka. *Chto chitat' o kommunisticheskoi morali* [What To Read on Communist Morals]. Moskva: Gos. Biblioteka SSSR im. V. I. Lenina, 1960. 83 pp.

Rebrin, V. A. *Obshchestvennyi dolg stroitelei kommunizma; kategoriia dolga v marksistsko-leninskoi etike* [The Social Duty of the Builder of Communism; The Category of Duty in Marxist-Leninist Ethics]. Novosibirsk: Zapadno-Sibirskoe Knizhnoe Izd., 1965. 363 pp.

Semenov, M. N. *O moral'nom avtoritete* [*On Moral Authority*]. Alma-Ata, 1967. 127 pp.

Shishkin, A. F. "Samaia spravedlivaia blagorodnaia moral' " [The Most Just and Noble Morality], *Kommunist* 1965, 3, 115-19.

Shvartsman, K. A. "Intuitivizm—odno iz proiavlenii krizisa burzhuaznoi eticheskoi mysli" [Intuitionism is One of the Manifestations of the Crisis of Bourgeois Ethical Thought], *Voprosy filosofii* 1962, 9, 88-99.

Sitnikov, E. M. "Kommunisticheskaia partiia—istoricheski neobkhodimoe uslovie preodoleniia 'otchuzhdeniia' cheloveka" [The Communist Party Is an Historically Necessary Condition of Overcoming the 'Alienation' of Man], *Filosofskie nauki* 1965, 6, 16-20.

Trubnikov, N. N. *O kategoriiakh "tsel'," "sredstvo," "rezul'tat"* [On the Categories "End," "Means," and "Result"]. Moskva: "Vysshaia Shkola," 1968. 148 pp.

"Trud i dolg sovetskogo uchenogo" [The Work and the Duty of the Soviet Scientist], *Kommunist* 1967, 3, 3-12.

Utkin, S. S. *Osnovy marksistsko-leninskoi etiki* [*Fundamentals of Marxist-Leninist Ethics*]. Rostov-na-Donu: Rostovskii GU, 1961. 240 pp.

"Vysokii dolg kommunista pered partiei i narodom" [The Highest Duty of a Communist Before the Party and the People], *Kommunist* 1964, 18, 3-11.

Index

Alexandrov, G., 4
Alienation, 1, 3, 32, 52, 156, 159
Angell, R.C., 132
Anti-Dühring, 2
Antigone, 101
Aristippus, 143
Aristotle, 8, 19, 49
Arkhangel'skii, L.M., 35, 177
Aurelius, M., 62
Authority, moral, 116-17
Ayer, A.J., 137

Base, economic, 15, 22-23, 128;
    of the Soviet Union, 21
Baskin, M.P., 131
Being, social, 14-15;
    and morality, 21
Being and Nothingness, 138
Bentham, J., 8
Bloch, E., 5

Capital, 1
Capitalism, crisis of, 129-33;
    remnants of, 100, 109
Carnap, R., 137
Category, 34-37, 177
Causality, 57-58, 64
Chermenina, A.P., 68-69
Choice, 65-68
Class, meaning of, 42
Code, moral, 7;
    of the builder of communism,
        2, 44, 77, 83-103, 105-106,
        112, 117, 122, 148, 163-64;
    Soviet, 22
Collectivism, 92-94, 140, 143-44
Communism, 10, 21, 28, 30, 54, 76,
        81, 146;
    building of, 6-7, 22, 120, 169;
    devotion to, 87-88;
    meaning, 40-43, 51, 88-89;
    as moral end, 29;
    as moral ideal, 27, 30-33, 39-46,
        48-50
Communist Party of the Soviet
    Union, 6, 80, 85;

and morality, 99, 112, 115-17,
    120-21;
    see also Program of the CPSU
Conscience, 19, 71, 77-80, 101, 121,
    148;
    autonomy of, 78;
    collective, 79-80;
    definition, 78;
    education of, 113;
    as ethical category, 35
Consciousness: lag of, 61, 84;
    social, 5, 14-15, 155
Control, social, 6, 19, 119-25, 148
Courts, comrades', 108, 168
Crisis, economic, 129-31;
    moral, 22, 129-33, 149-50
Criterion, moral, 39-40, 43-44
Critique de la raison dialectique,
    138
Critique of the Gotha Program, 1
Custom and morality, 16-17

Descartes, R., 8
Determinism, 57-70;
    definition, 57;
    economic, 59-63;
    in history, 3-4;
    mechanistic, 58;
    psychological, 67-68
Dewey, J., 138
Divorce, 96
Djilas, M., 42
Drobnitskii, O.G., 177
Duty, 74-76, 112;
    and conscience, 77-78;

definition, 28;
  as ethical category, 35;
  and good, 74;
  military, 109-10, 169;
  objectivity of, 75;
  public, 92

*Economic and Philosophic Manu-
    scripts of 1844*, 1, 6
Education, moral, 113-14, 144-45
End of man, 27, 33, 146-47
Engels, F., 1, 2, 5-7, 14, 20-22, 28-
    30, 40, 48, 121, 139
Epictetus, 62
Equality, 42, 45, 49, 102
Ethics: bourgeois, 6, 133-41;
    Christian, 13;
    definition, 13;
    natural law, 13;
    objectivist, 28;
    revisionist, 6
Ethics Without Morality, 128
Evaluation, moral, 80-81
Evolutionism, Darwinian, 13
Existentialism, 134-135, 137-38
Exploitation, 51, 141

Fallacy, naturalistic, 36
Family, 96-98
Fedorenko, E.G., 81
Feuerbach, L., 29, 52, 139
Freedom, 3, 11, 49-50, 57-70, 143-
    44, 160;
    and responsibility, 71
Freudianism, 72

Good, 34-55;
    and duty, 74;
    as ethical category, 34-39;
    meaning, 28, 35, 37, 63
Gumnitskii, G.K., 35, 37

Happiness, 49-50;
    as ethical category, 35
Hare, R., 137
Hegel, G.W.F., 52, 139
History, materialist conception of,
    13, 27, 120; *see also* Material-
    ism, historical
*History of West-European Philos-
    ophy*, 4
Holy Family, The, 1
Honesty, 95
Honor, 35
Humanism, 3, 6, 95, 103, 138

Ideal, moral, 34-35, 124; *see also*
    Communism
Idealism, 134
Ideology, 7, 14
Il'ichev, L.F., 106
Imperative, categorical, 18-19
Inculcation, moral, 112, 177; mo-
    rality of, 118-19
Individual and society, 10, 37-38,
    100
Individualism, 134, 143
Indoctrination, moral, 109
Integration, moral, 132-133

James, W., 138
Justice, 3, 45, 49-50, 81, 102

Kalinin, M.I., 109
Kant, I., 8, 19, 36, 122, 135
Kharchev, A.G., 177
Khrushchev, N.S., 113, 140, 163
Kierkegaard, S., 8
Kolakowski, L., 7
Kollontai, A., 96

Labor, 89-92, 110, 177;
    division of, 3, 19, 31-32, 52, 156
Laplace, P.S., 57

Law, 111;
   and morality, 25, 89, 107-109
Laws: of nature, 28, 59;
   of social development, 22-33, 142
Lenin, V.I., 1, 2, 7, 22, 40, 96, 110,
   120, 124, 129, 139
Ludwig Feuerbach, 2
Lukacs, G., 7

Makarenko, A.S., 114
Man: collectivist view, 3, 31, 33,
   142-43, 149;
   and labor, 90;
   nature of, 14-15, 48, 53;
   personalistic view, 143-144;
   Soviet view, 29-33
*Manifesto of the Communist
   Party,* 96
Marx, K., 1, 2, 6-7, 9-10, 14, 19-22,
   28-30, 32, 40-41, 48, 120-121,
   129, 139, 150; and determinism, 59-60, 62; and ethics,
   2-4
Materialism, historical, 5, 13, 15,
   135;
   and morality, 15;
   see also History, materialist
      conception of
Mead, M., 17
Metaethics, 6, 14, 136-37, 154
Mill, J.S., 8, 49, 135
Moore, G.E., 35-36, 135
Moral Code of the Builder of
   Communism, *see* Code
Morality: all-human, 23-24, 87,
   117, 124, 150;
   autonomous, 122-123;
   bourgeois, 21, 127;
   Christian, 8-9;
   class, 20-21, 119;
   communist, 10, 14, 21, 24, 85, 87,
      124, 150, 177;

conformity, 121-23, 140;
definition, 14, 16, 25, 35, 119,
   155;
functional role of, 111-12;
lag of, 21-22, 26, 84;
and law, 107-109;
manipulative, 121-23;
military, 109-10;
objectivity of, 17-18;
origin of, 16-17, 24-25, 37-38,
   155;
proletarian, 21;
relative independence of, 21-23,
   60-62;
sexual, 167;
socialist, 84, 150
Moses, 87
Motive, 68, 71, 80

Nietzsche, F., 8, 19
Nihilism, 137
Neopositivism, 134-37, 154
Neo-Thomism, 134-135, 138

Obligation, *prima facie,* 76-77
O tsennostiakh zhizni i kul'tury,
   10

Parasitism, 91, 98, 109
Paternalism, 99, 102, 115-16, 167
Patriotism, 88-89
Pavlov, I.P., 114
Peirce, C.S., 138
Person, 100-102, 144
Philosopher, moral, 8-11, 19-20
Pragmatism, 13, 134-135, 138
Principia Ethica, 35
Principles, moral, 44, 54, 86-87,
   105, 113, 124
Production, means and modes of,
   15, 30, 145

Program of the CPSU, 6, 9, 40-41,
51, 83, 87, 106, 129, 163-64;
see also Communist Party of
the Soviet Union
Property, private, 3, 32, 141, 145-
46, 156
Provincialism, 102
Punishment, 81;
capital, 92, 139-40

Reason, 19, 29
Refutation, 6;
of non-Marxist ethics, 128-141,
177
Relativism, 134, 137;
ethical, 13, 17-18
Religion, 51
Reminiscences, 96
Responsibility, 3, 70-74, 101, 110,
118;
collective, 72-74, 79-80
Revisionism, 135, 138
Right, definition, 28
Rights, 81, 102, 143, 163

Sartre, J-P., 137-138
Schaff, A., 105
Self-realization, 28-29
Sex and morality, 96-97

Shishkin, A.F., 35, 130, 177
Shvartsman, K.A., 128, 131, 177
Socialism, 53, 69
Stalin, J., 4-6, 116
Stevenson, C., 137
Sumner, W., 17
Superstructure, social, 62;
active role of, 5-6, 85;
and morality, 1,5;
relative independence of, 5

Teleology, 28
Tugarinov, V.P., 10, 36, 81, 177

Unity, moral-political, 6, 89
Utilitarianism, 8, 13, 28

Value, theory of, 6, 33, 46-48, 153,
156-57, 177
Values: communist, 148;
externalization of, 100-101;
and facts, 39, 46-47;
incompatibility of, 10;
social, 132

Will, 68
Work, *see* Labor

Zetkin, C., 96
Zhdanov, A.A., 4

STUDIES OF THE RUSSIAN INSTITUTE

PUBLISHED BY COLUMBIA UNIVERSITY PRESS

THAD PAUL ALTON, *Polish Postwar Economy*

JOHN A. ARMSTRONG, *Ukrainian Nationalism*

ABRAM BERGSON, *Soviet National Income and Product in 1937*

EDWARD J. BROWN, *The Proletarian Episode in Russian Literature, 1928–1932*

HARVEY L. DYCK, *Weimar Germany and Soviet Russia, 1926–1933: A Study in Diplomatic Instability*

RALPH TALCOTT FISHER, JR., *Pattern for Soviet Youth: A Study of the Congresses of the Komsomol, 1918–1954*

MAURICE FRIEDBERG, *Russian Classics in Soviet Jackets*

ELLIOT R. GOODMAN, *The Soviet Design for a World State*

DAVID GRANICK, *Management of the Industrial Firm in the USSR: A Study in Soviet Economic Planning*

THOMAS TAYLOR HAMMOND, *Lenin on Trade Unions and Revolution, 1893–1917*

JOHN N. HAZARD, *Settling Disputes in Soviet Society: The Formative Years of Legal Institutions*

DAVID JORAVSKY, *Soviet Marxism and Natural Science, 1917–1932*

DAVID MARSHALL LANG, *The Last Years of the Georgian Monarchy, 1658–1832*

GEORGE S. N. LUCKYJ, *Literary Politics in the Soviet Ukraine, 1917-1934*

HERBERT MARCUSE, *Soviet Marxism: A Critical Analysis*

KERMIT E. MCKENZIE, *Comintern and World Revolution, 1928–1943: The Shaping of Doctrine*

CHARLES B. MCLANE, *Soviet Policy and the Chinese Communists, 1931–1946*

JAMES WILLIAM MORLEY, *The Japanese Thrust into Siberia, 1918*

ALEXANDER G. PARK, *Bolshevism in Turkestan, 1917–1927*

MICHAEL BORO PETROVICH, *The Emergence of Russian Panslavism, 1856–1870*

OLIVER H. RADKEY, *The Agrarian Foes of Bolshevism: Promise and Default of the Russian Socialist Revolutionaries, February to October, 1917*

OLIVER H. RADKEY, *The Sickle Under the Hammer: The Russian Socialist Revolutionaries in the Early Months of Soviet Rule*

ALFRED J. RIEBER, *Stalin and the French Communist Party, 1941–1947*

ALFRED ERICH SENN, *The Emergence of Modern Lithuania*

ERNEST J. SIMMONS, editor, *Through the Glass of Soviet Literature: Views of Russian Society*

THEODORE K. VON LAUE, *Sergei Witte and the Industrialization of Russia*

ALLEN S. WHITING, *Soviet Policies in China, 1917–1924*

PUBLISHED BY TEACHERS COLLEGE PRESS

HAROLD J. NOAH, *Financing Soviet Schools*

PUBLISHED BY PRINCETON UNIVERSITY PRESS

PAUL AVRICH, *The Russian Anarchists*

ROBERT A. MAGUIRE, *Red Virgin Soil: Soviet Literature in the 1920's*

JOHN M. THOMPSON, *Russia, Bolshevism, and the Versailles Peace*